Above A fishing boat in the mouth of the River Esk
at Whitby heads out to sea.

Following page A classic Dales scene of an ancient
walled track leading down through the rich green
pastures of Upper Wharfedale to the village of
Thorpe-sub-Montem.

YORKSHIRE

A PORTRAIT IN COLOUR

TEXT BY DUNCAN SMITH
PHOTOGRAPHS BY TREVOR CROUCHER

THE DOVECOTE PRESS

For Mary, Trevor, Catherine, Adrian and Eva
For Susan

One of the many fine brass bands from around Yorkshire and the North of England who participate in the celebrated Hardraw Brass Band Contest, which takes place every September in a magnificent natural amphitheatre in front of Hardraw Force in Wensleydale. The original playing of brass instruments in both lead and coal mining areas is thought to have been encouraged as a way of excercising the lungs.

First published in 1995 by The Dovecote Press Ltd
Stanbridge, Wimborne, Dorset BH21 4JD

ISBN 1 874336 33 4

Photographs © Trevor Croucher 1995
Text © Duncan Smith 1995

Designed and produced by The Dovecote Press Ltd
Photoset in Sabon by The Typesetting Bureau, Wimborne, Dorset
Printed and bound in Singapore

British Library Cataloguing-in-Publication Data
A Catalogue record of this book is
available from the British Library

1 3 5 7 9 10 8 6 4 2

CONTENTS

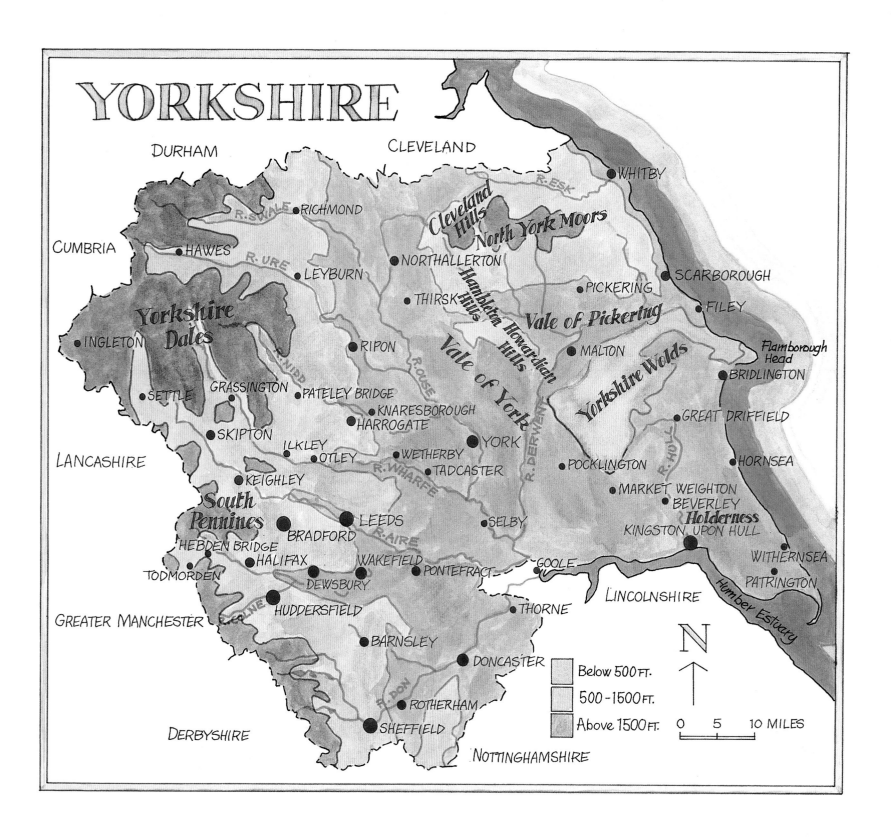

YORKSHIRE

DURHAM

CLEVELAND

CUMBRIA

LANCASHIRE

GREATER MANCHESTER

DERBYSHIRE

NOTTINGHAMSHIRE

LINCOLNSHIRE

R. ESK

• WHITBY

Cleveland Hills

North York Moors

• RICHMOND

R. SWALE

• HAWES

R. URE

• LEYBURN

• NORTHALLERTON

• THIRSK

Hambleton Hills

Howardian Hills

Vale of Pickering

• PICKERING

• SCARBOROUGH

• FILEY

Yorkshire Dales

• INGLETON

• RIPON

R. NIDD

• MALTON

Flamborough Head

• BRIDLINGTON

Vale of York

R. OUSE

Yorkshire Wolds

• SETTLE

GRASSINGTON

• PATELEY BRIDGE

• KNARESBOROUGH

HARROGATE

• GREAT DRIFFIELD

• SKIPTON

ILKLEY

• OTLEY

• WETHERBY

• YORK

R. DERWENT

• POCKLINGTON

R. HULL

• HORNSEA

• KEIGHLEY

R. WHARFE

• TADCASTER

• MARKET WEIGHTON

• BEVERLEY

Holderness

South Pennines

• LEEDS

R. AIRE

• SELBY

KINGSTON UPON HULL

HEBDEN BRIDGE

BRADFORD

• WITHERNSEA

HALIFAX

WAKEFIELD

GOOLE

• PATRINGTON

TODMORDEN

DEWSBURY

• PONTEFRACT

Humber Estuary

R. COLNE

HUDDERSFIELD

• THORNE

• BARNSLEY

• DONCASTER

Below 500 FT.

500 - 1500 FT.

Above 1500 FT.

N

R. DON

• ROTHERHAM

• SHEFFIELD

0   5   10 MILES

YORKSHIRE

As England's largest county, and with a population of nearly five million, Yorkshire is often described as 'the county of broad acres' and 'most renowned of Shires'. Neither its size or renown are in doubt, but it is worth remembering that its boundaries contain three sub-counties, the thousand year old Viking 'Ridings' of North, West and East Yorkshire. In 1974 the councils bearing those names were abolished and the county was reorganised. Sedbergh and Dent were lost to Cumbria and Barnoldswick to Lancashire, whilst two thirds of the old West Riding was split into the new smaller regions of West and South Yorkshire. Most of the old East Riding was controversially linked with North Lincolnshire into the new Humberside; whilst the remainder was absorbed into a sprawling North Yorkshire. Twenty-one years later, and even as I write, ancient loyalties and commonsense have brought the Government close to partially reinstating the old divisions.

Yorkshire is roughly square in shape, and bounded by the Pennine uplands to the west and North Sea to the east. South lie the Humber Estuary and Derbyshire Peak District, whilst to the north are the River Tees and Cleveland Hills. The county's great rivers drain the entire county and form an integral part of the Yorkshire scene, from the clear, gushing hillside 'beck' to the steady, navigable river. Indeed Yorkshire's waterways embrace much of its life and industry. Up them sailed the first Viking settlers, whilst from the Middle Ages onwards they served as the arteries down which flowed the raw materials and goods that brought the county its wealth.

Yorkshire reaches its greatest height amid the high limestone Dales and fells of Richmondshire and Craven; James Herriott's 'land of pure air, rocky streams and hidden waterfalls'. This is peerless wild countryside, with a trio of great Pennine peaks, white limestone scars and pavements, solitary barns, long ribbons of drystone walls switchbacking their way up and down dale, as well as an underground maze of potholes and caverns. Here are Swaledale and Wensleydale, whilst to the south are remote Nidderdale and the delightful Craven Dales of Upper Wharfedale, Malhamdale and renegade Ribblesdale, whose river is the only one in the county that fails to flow east to the North Sea.

The limestone that created the Dales was once buried beneath a thick deposit of sandstone. Massive earth movements and glacial scouring re-exposed the limestone, largely restricting the sandstone to the characteristic gritstone caps of the high fells. But to the south-east the sandstone has survived as Millstone Grit, dominating the landscape throughout Mid-Wharfedale, Airedale, Calderdale and the Colne Valley. This South Pennine area has long been Yorkshire's commercial backbone, most notably in the production of textiles. In the late eighteenth century the hill-village hand-knitters and weavers were made redundant by mechanical water-driven looms. The advent of steam led to a gradual migration into the valleys, and by the end of the nineteenth century smoke from the chimneys of Leeds, Bradford, Halifax and Huddersfield darkened the skyline. Still further to the south, in the Don Valley, charcoal had been smelted to turn local iron ore into steel since as early as the fourteenth century, a process greatly accelerated by the mining of the vast coal measures which overlie the gritstone in South and West Yorkshire. This is the 'Black Country', where in the eighteenth century the ready availability of coal, iron and running water was the catalyst for an Industrial Revolution that has shaped much of its subsequent history.

The centre of the county is dissected by the finger-like Vale of York, scoured out by primeval glaciers. Running north to south, and only a hundred feet above sea level at its highest point, the Vale's fertile alluvial soil made it some of the richest farming land in the county. Crops and cattle brought wealth to its landowners, who in turn left to their heirs an architectural legacy of country-houses, mansions and stately homes that still endures. In the heart of the Vale is Yorkshire's capital, with its spectacular Minster and ancient city walls. The south-eastern corner of the county offers yet another of the contrasts that give Yorkshire its variety. The long crumbling coastline, ending at Spurn Point, is constantly on the move and threatened by erosion, whilst inland from Holderness are the rolling arable chalk lands of the Wolds, Yorkshire's 'breadbasket', which in turn come to an abrupt end on the coast at Flamborough Head.

North of the Wolds the land falls away into the Vale of Pickering, with its bustling market towns and villages, before climbing again to the expansive tableland of the North York Moors. Although often thought of as bleak and windswept, the moors boast dozens of little dales whose green swathes cut through the purple heather and 'vacant wine-red moors' that form the heights. In the extreme east the Moors collapse into the sea, creating a rugged coastline where charming, pantiled fishing villages cling to the cliffs, and holiday resorts such as Scarborough throng with visitors throughout the summer.

The tides of history have swept to and fro over much of Yorkshire, leaving in their wake evidence of all the major periods in Britain's past and proving that it was always a prize worth fighting for. The moors are still dotted with the standing stones and burial mounds of the first settlers. The native tribe of the Brigantes put up fierce resistance against the Romans who, in turn, left a series of camps, towns and coastal signal stations as well as miles of straight paved roads. The fifth century saw the invasion of the Anglo-Saxons from across the North Sea, and by the ninth and tenth centuries they had been followed by the Vikings. Yorkshire's spirit of rebellion and independence cost it dearly under the early years of Norman rule, but the new conquerors left the county its superb array of castles, abbeys and cathedrals. Finally came the Civil Wars, the creation of the great landed estates, the Industrial Revolution with its railways and canals, and, more recently, the realization that Yorkshire could offer both residents and visitors a range of landscapes and a historical heritage without equal in England. All those who have crossed Yorkshire's borders have been struck by the beauty and strong, sobering character of the place. But it is ultimately the intense and forthright spirit of the Yorkshire folk themselves which unifies the seemingly disparate topography of this vast county. It is precisely this 'spirit' which photographer Trevor Croucher has captured so successfully. His work is all the more important as the bland uniformity of modern times increasingly threatens the integrity and character of the old Shires of England. It is hoped that this book will bear witness to the people and landscape of a still proud and beautiful county.

DUNCAN SMITH, *Sheffield*

SWALEDALE AND WENSLEYDALE

SWALEDALE AND WENSLEYDALE

*'. . . the finest countryside in Britain, with their magnificent clean
and austere outbursts of hill and moor, their charming villages and
remote white-washed farms, their astonishing variety of aspect and
appeal, from the gaunt rocks down to the twinkling rivers.'*
The Dalesman, 1939

THUS did the Bradford-born writer J. B. Priestley sum-up the attractions of the limestone Dales in Yorkshire's north-western corner. Nowhere are Priestley's words more obvious than in Swaledale and Wensleydale, where workaday settlements with ancient market charters cluster along the river banks. As the valleys broaden, lush meadows sway with buttercups, clover and cranesbill. The hillsides support stands of ash, rowan and wild rose, while on the high open moorland grouse and pipits pick their way amongst tufts of white-flowering cloudberry, and the only sounds are the bleating of sheep, the shrill piping of the golden plover and the curlew's desolate cry.

Swaledale is high and remote. The search for lead brought the Romans to its grey glacial fells, although it was not until the eighteenth and nineteenth centuries that the industry reached its peak. Farmers sought their fortunes as miners and quiet hamlets echoed to the hooves of lines of pack horses. Swaledale lead ended up on the roofs of churches and cathedrals as far away as Rome. By the late nineteenth century cheap imports had brought the boom to an end. With no prospects hundreds of former miners moved away to the mill towns of West Yorkshire and the economy of the area once again became dependent on sheep and hill farming. Beyond Grinton the dale becomes gentler, with the ruins of several religious houses standing close to the banks of the Swale. The entrance to Swaledale is guarded by the great Norman keep at Richmond and the military presence continues to this day with army camps and practice ranges on the hills between Richmond and Leyburn in Wensleydale.

Wensleydale is unusual amongst the Dales in being named after a village rather than its river, the Ure. The river rises amongst the peat of Mallerstang Edge, close to the Cumbria border, but from Appersett, where several small dales converge, down to the market town of Leyburn, it flows through a broad fertile valley with expansive green pastures on its slopes. The upper dale still feels pleasantly old fashioned in its 'capital', Hawes, where rope-making has survived the older industries of knitting, mining and quarrying. Downstream, Bainbridge – where there was a Roman fort – still celebrates the ancient custom of blowing horns to guide travellers lost in the former Forest of Wensleydale. Nearby Aysgarth has some of the Dales' finest waterfalls, while lonely Bishopdale was once a royal hunting preserve under the protection of Bolton Castle.

Beyond Wensley, depopulated by the Black Death in 1346-48, the land becomes a rolling mixture of park and farmland. The town of Middleham, with its imposing ruined

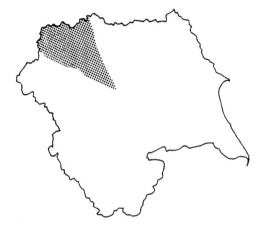

Previous page The Cauldron Falls on Walden Beck close to the village of West Burton in Wensleydale, noted for having one of the largest village greens in England. This is a typical waterfall in these northern Dales, the water cutting its way through the succession of hard limestones and softer sandstones and shales to form a series of steps.

Right Looking north along the Buttertubs Pass, which crosses the watershed between Wensleydale and Swaledale to Kisdon Hill. Once only a rough track, the road affords superb views as it climbs from Hawes in Wensleydale, passing between the high fells of Lovely Seat and Great Shunner Fell, before dropping into Swaledale near Thwaite. The Buttertubs themselves are a series of natural fluted limestone shafts up to 100 feet deep, and probably owe their name to the fact that they were used by farmers to store unsold butter until the next market.

Castle, has long been known as the 'Newmarket of the North' because of its racehorse gallops and the many stables that use them. A little further downstream lie the peaceful ruins of Jervaulx Abbey, whose monks bred horses and – in common with those of other Cistercian houses – turned ewes' milk into a cheese that bears the name of the Dale to this day. Beyond Jervaulx, the River Ure leaves Wensleydale in favour of the open countryside around Masham and West Tanfield before turning south towards the soaring landmark of Ripon's magnificent cathedral.

Looking down Upper Swaledale towards Muker, a village where Muker Beck and the River Swale meet. Each of the surrounding walled fields, many of which are fine hay meadows, still retain their characteristic barns for winter shelter and feed storage. The influence of Scandinavian settlers in the area is evident from the Norse names of Muker ('meadow'), Keld ('spring'), and Thwaite ('clearing'). They were all linked not only by lead mining in the nineteenth century but physically by the medieval Corpse Road down the dale to Grinton where the dead were buried prior to the consecration of a burial ground at Muker.

Gunnerside Gill in Upper Swaledale, its Old Norse name meaning 'Gunnar's pasture'. Nowhere in Britain can the pattern of walled pastures and hay barns be seen better than here. However, it was at the height of the lead mining industry during the eighteenth and nineteenth centuries that Swaledale saw its greatest prosperity, and the mines in Gunnerside Gill were amongst the most productive. Note how the slopes are scarred by 'hushes', where dammed water was released to strip away the soil to reveal ore-bearing rock. The two main local mines, Lownathwaite and Blakethwaite, produced lead well into the nineteenth century.

The ruined Surrender Smelt Mill of 1839 in Old Gang Beck, an area scattered with the remains of once booming lead mines. The ruined engine houses, smelt mills, peat stores and tunnels that still survive first began to close in the 1870s when cheap imports led to a decline in the industry. The C.B. Hotel in nearby Arkengarthdale is named after Charles Bathurst, who bought the manor in 1656 and developed lead mining in the local dales.

The massive Norman ramparts of Richmond Castle which tower over the market town of Richmond and guard the entrance to Swaledale. The Castle was begun in 1071 by Earl Alan the Red of Brittany, who had been given the vast Honour of Richmond as a reward for his part in William the Conqueror's Harrying of the North two years earlier. Despite its great strength, the Castle was never besieged, and remains remarkably intact. Defended by its castle, and made prosperous by the tradesmens' guilds that were established in the wake of a regular market, Richmond matured into the commercial capital of the Dale. In the huge cobbled Market Square is the twelfth century Holy Trinity Church which now serves as a regimental museum for the Green Howards, associated with Richmond since 1875 when both a depot and barracks were opened in the town. Richmond is an architectural delight. Its Georgian past includes the Theatre Royal, built in 1788, and the only theatre of its age to survive in its original condition.

Above A field barn tucked into the corner of a field near Simonstone in Upper Wensleydale with Cotter Fell End in the background. The barns are a characteristic feature of the northern dales, as are the drystone walls that surround them. Their original function was to provide winter shelter for sheep and cattle, whose hay was stored in lofts above. Although many have fallen derelict, some are still in use, whilst others have been renovated as homes or as 'bunk-barns' for visitors.

Left Hand-filling cheese moulds with freshly shredded curd in the cheeseroom at the celebrated Wensleydale Creamery in Hawes. The earliest record of cheesemaking in the dale dates to Norman times when the Cistercian monks at Jervaulx Abbey began turning milk from their ewes into cheese. Farmers' wives continued the tradition until 1897 when a corn merchant in Hawes began production on a larger scale. By 1992 the Milk Marketing Board had taken control and threatened to transfer the business to Lancashire, causing considerable uproar and an eventual management buyout. Using milk from cows in the surrounding pastures, traditional handmade Wensleydale cheese is again in production in Hawes, providing a traditional accompaniment to fruit cake and apple pie.

Looking across Semerwater in Raydale, a tributary valley joining Wensleydale at Bainbridge, towards the distinctive flat-topped fells of Addleborough and Penhill. Semerwater is fed by three streams and is Yorkshire's third largest freshwater lake after Hornsea Mere and Malham Tarn, whilst the two mile long River Bain it feeds is England's shortest river.

Aysgarth Falls in Wensleydale, formed where the previously placid River Ure cascades over three flights of wide limestone steps in a wooded gorge. In the past the river powered a woollen mill, now a coaching museum, which in the 1860s supplied the material for 7,000 red flannel shirts for the soldiers of Garibaldi's Italian army.

The unmistakable ruins of Bolton Castle in Wensleydale with its commanding views up Bishopdale (right) and Walden (left). It was built by Richard le Scrope, Lord High Chancellor of England, between 1379-99 to defend the Dale against the Scots. Bolton Castle was the last of the great medieval castles to be built in Yorkshire and is, in effect, more a heavily fortified house than a fortress. The Scropes were an influential family, producing numerous distinguished statesmen, lawyers and clerics. In the 1560s Mary Queen of Scots was held here in considerable luxury on her slow journey southwards to execution. During the Civil War the Castle was held for the King by Colonel Chaytor until the occupants were starved out by Cromwell's Parliamentarians in 1645, after which one of its four towers was demolished, rendering it defenceless. A museum and restaurant are now housed in part of the remains, but only a century ago it was lived in by 13 separate families, many of them lead miners.

Farrier Dougie Jemmeson shoeing a racehorse in the shadow of Middleham Castle. Racing stables have existed in the town for 200 years, whilst horses were first bred in Wensleydale by the medieval monks at nearby Jervaulx Abbey. The twelfth century castle was owned by Richard Neville, Earl of Warwick, and earned the title of the 'Windsor of the North', so frequent were the visits of medieval monarchs. It is most famous as the home of Richard, Duke of Gloucester, later Richard III, who was made Lord of the North by his elder brother Edward IV. He obtained Middleham Castle through marriage in 1472 to the Earl's daughter, Anne Neville, occupying it during the Wars of the Roses. Once one of the strongest fortresses in the north, it became untenanted in the late fifteenth century, and much of its stonework was incorporated into buildings in the town.

The busy market town of Leyburn, perched high above the Ure in Wensleydale and recorded in Domesday Book as 'Leborne', or 'the stream by the forest clearing'. Leyburn owes its growth to an outbreak of plague in nearby Wensley, the dale's namesake, which in 1563 was reduced to a cluster of houses. Leyburn was granted a market by Charles II, which is still held on a Friday in a square dominated by the Victorian Town Hall given to the town by the then lord of the manor, Lord Bolton. Above the town is Leyburn Shawl, a natural terrace running parallel with the valley and affording a fine panorama of the dale. A spot known as 'Queen's Gap' is said to be where Mary Queen of Scots was recaptured after only two hours of freedom during her imprisonment in Bolton Castle.

Above West Tanfield near Ripon, viewed across the River Ure, and dominated by St Nicholas' Church, parts of which date to Norman times. It contains tombs and memorials to the Marmions who came here in 1215 and built the Castle, of which only the medieval gatehouse – with its lovely oriel window – remains. Behind the Castle, and just visible between it and the church, is Tanfield Hall, once home to Miss Elizabeth Clarke who in 1871 married Colonel Rookes Everly Bell Crompton. He lit the Hall by a water-powered generator and, on moving to London, did the same not only for his own house but also Buckingham Palace and Windsor Castle. Fame and fortune came after he illuminated the city of Vienna.

Left The peaceful ruins of the Chapter House of Jervaulx Abbey, set in sheep-grazed parkland on the banks of the River Ure. It was established in 1156 by Cistercians monks, who, according to one legend, were led there from a bleak site near Askrigg by a small boy bearing a branch. The Abbey eventually became the largest landowner in Wensleydale, but in 1538 it was ransacked by Henry VIII after the last Abbot, Adam Sedbergh, was hanged on Tyburn Hill in 1537 for his reluctant part in the Pilgrimage of Grace, an ill-fated protest against the closure of religious houses. Much of the fine honey-coloured sandstone was taken away, but enough remains to recognize the outline of some of the buildings, including the fifteenth century kitchen and infirmary.

Fountains Abbey, near Ripon, regarded as the finest monastic ruin in Western Europe, was founded in 1132 by thirteen monks who seceded from the Benedictines at York Abbey. Although opting for the stricter Cistercian way of life, the Abbey became the wealthiest and most powerful in Britain due to its involvement in the lead, iron and wool trades. The monks possessed vast areas of land as far as Penyghent, high in the Pennines. On the right is the vaulted cellar where fleeces were stored, which at 300 feet long is the largest of its kind in Europe. After the Dissolution in 1539 the Abbey was ransacked and by 1699 had passed to John Aislabie of Studley Royal, a former Chancellor of the Exchequer. Together with his son William they combined their estates to form a landscaped park dotted with ornaments, the largest of which was the Abbey itself. Others include the Banqueting House by Colin Campbell, the Temple of Fame and the Temple of Piety, renamed by William as a filial gesture soon after his father's death in 1742. By damming the River Skell they created the famous Studley Royal Water Gardens, now designated a World Heritage Site.

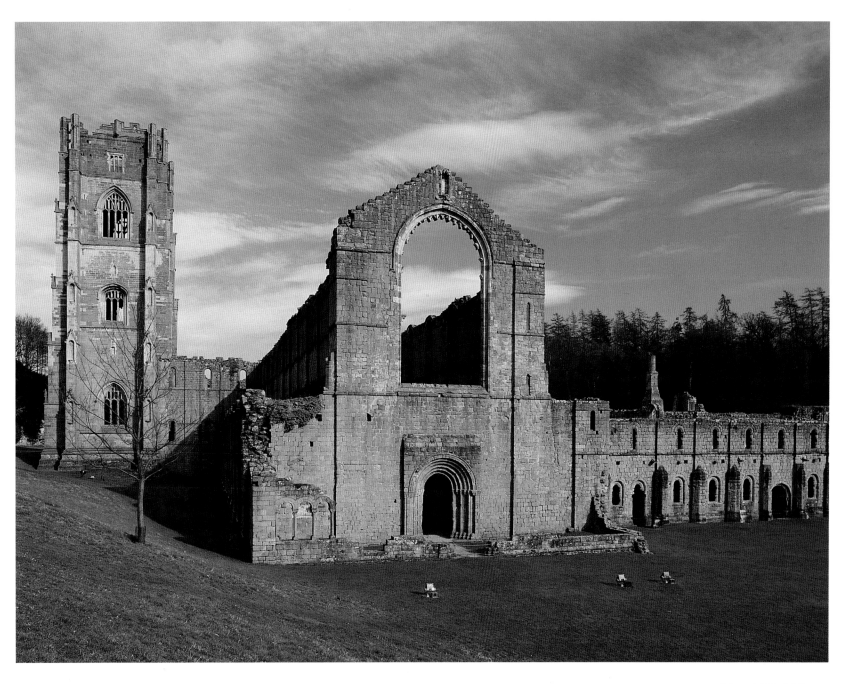

Yorkshire's only fortified manor house to have survived intact to this day, Markenfield Hall, near Ripon, was built by Chancellor of the Exchequer John de Markenfield in about 1310 when he received his 'license to crenellate'. More due to its seclusion than its strength, the moated house even escaped damage during the Scots' incursion south after their victory at Bannockburn in 1314. However, the family lost their home and estate, like many other Yorkshire Catholics, after supporting Mary Stuart's claim to the throne during the abortive Rising of the North in 1569. Queen Elizabeth I granted the hall to her Lord Keeper, Sir Thomas Egerton, who built the gatehouse. In 1782 it was sold to Baron Grantley, and it is now amicably shared between the 7th Lord Grantley and his tenants.

'St Wilfred', on horseback, and his attendant monks parading through the streets of Ripon during the Saint's annual feast in August. A Northumbrian by birth, in 686 AD Wilfred had walked from exile in Rome back to Ripon where he built the first church. In medieval times this was celebrated by carrying his effigy out of the city, returning with it on the same day. Today a citizen of Ripon plays the part of the saint and the procession winds its way from the Town Hall to the Cathedral, accompanied by floats, bands and the City of Ripon Morris Dancers. Behind the 'saint' is the Ripon Wakeman, a chief official in days before the mayor existed, who sounds a curfew horn in the Market Square to announce that the city is in his care for the night.

THE CRAVEN DALES
AND NIDDERDALE

THE CRAVEN DALES
AND NIDDERDALE

THE name 'Craven' has been translated as the *land of the crags*, and no name could be more apt. Covering the Wenning Valley and the upland areas of Ribblesdale, Malhamdale and Upper Wharfedale, the area is acknowledged as containing the finest limestone scenery in the county.

The Ribble rises on the same bleak and peaty moorland of Cam Fell that gives birth to the Wharfe. The dale head – one of the wildest and most spectacular spots in the Dales – is overshadowed by the massive 2,414 feet high bulk of Whernside, making the Ribblehead Viaduct that carries the Settle-Carlisle Railway into Cumbria look almost insignificant. The old-world villages of Horton-in-Ribblesdale, Clapham and Ingleton are bases for climbing the Three Peaks of Ingleborough, Penyghent and Whernside, as well as important centres for caving and potholing. Settle, a favourite of the composer Elgar, marks the gateway to the Dale, and south of it the Ribble flows across the Craven Basin into Lancashire. Around the village of Malham are former cotton mills, lead, zinc and coal mines in a dale once shared by the monks of Fountains Abbey and Bolton Priory. Scottish cattle drovers were frequent visitors to the great sales here and sheep remain important to this day. The arrival of the Leeds-Liverpool Canal at Skipton and Gargrave enabled the produce of the dale to be exported to both Lancashire and the industrial towns further down the River Aire.

From the heights of Cam Fell the becks that form the Ribble flow south; whilst a short distance away those which merge into the Wharfe head east as Oughtershaw Beck and flow through Langstrothdale Chase, the medieval hunting preserve described by Chaucer as being 'farre in the north can I not tell where'. In the vicinity of Yockenthwaite the young Wharfe runs through a strikingly-exposed bed of water-worn limestone, whilst in the main valley the combined force of the Wharfedale and Littondale glaciers have undercut the thick limestone outcrop to form the spectacular Kilnsey Crag. Kilnsey itself was a sheep farm (or 'grange') for Fountains Abbey, as was Arncliffe in Littondale. The long history of the occupation of the dale is everywhere apparent, for the bones of prehistoric animals have been found in caves such as Stump Cross. Elsewhere Saxon, Viking and Norman remains are found in many of the ancient churches. After passing the majestic ruins of the once-powerful Bolton Priory the river flows on to the broader regions of Mid-Wharfedale.

Nidderdale, the last of the great southern Dales, differs markedly from its neighbours in that the characteristic limestone scenery of so many of the Dales is replaced by the darker Millstone Grit. The River Nidd rises in the lee of Great and Little Whernside, a remote backwater of high grouse moor. Further down the dale the villages of Lofthouse

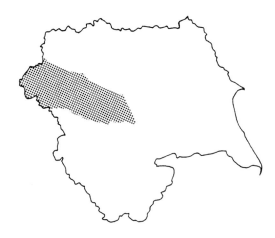

Previous page A prize-winning 'Dalesbred' ram (or 'tup') which, along with Swaledale and Scottish Blackface, are popular breeds on northern hills. The Dalesbred is identified by the two white spots, or 'smits', between the nostril and eyes. Hardy sheep, whose long, curly fleeces help insulate them against the worst of the Pennine winters, a champion ram can fetch many thousands of pounds at auction as a source of breeding stock. The horns of both the tups and ewes are greatly prized by walking-stick makers.

and Ramsgill began life as monastic granges of Fountains and Byland Abbeys, but the monks who once farmed them would find much of their surroundings unrecognizable, for the construction of reservoirs in the late nineteenth and early twentieth centuries has transformed the dale into a miniature Lake District. Greenhow, with its cluster of cottages and windswept church perched at 1,300 feet on the watershed between Nidderdale and Upper Wharfedale, is one of England's highest villages and a source of lead since as early as the Roman occupation. West of the old market town of Pateley Bridge the curiously weathered gritstone tors of Brimham Rocks are one of the area's biggest attractions. Leaving the Dales country the Nidd flows into the Vale of York through the gorge at Knaresborough – the administrative centre of the ancient Royal Forest of Knaresborough – close by the elegant spa town of Harrogate.

Right A party of schoolchildren at the foot of Thornton Force, a magnificent 46 feet waterfall, on the River Twiss north of Ingleton. The village of Ingleton was a coal mining and quarrying community which embraced tourism with the arrival of the railway in 1849. The peak of Ingleborough was the initial attraction, but in 1884 the virtually unknown wooded glens of the Twiss and the Doe, which join at Ingleton to form the Greta, were also made accessible to visitors. The rivers cross a series of faults revealing, beneath the Great Scar Limestone, the oldest rocks in the Dales, laid down some 400 million years ago.

Left The little hamlet of Feizor, nestling beneath Smearsett and Pot Scars in the Wenning Valley (a tributary of the Lune), is one of the prettiest in the limestone Dales. Hidden at the end of a lane off the main Settle to Ingleton road, one of its cottages contains a 'chimney-seat' to encourage visiting witches to remain outside the house.

Above A spectacular vista, from the juniper-clad summit of Moughton above Horton in Ribblesdale, of the snow-capped high fells of Upper Ribblesdale and the border of Cumbria. From right to left they are Cam Fell, Widdale Fell, Blea Moor, Wild Boar Fell (20 miles away), Baugh Fell, Whernside (2414 feet) and Park Fell.

Right The mighty 24-arched Ribblehead Viaduct carrying the recently rescued Settle-Carlisle Railway across the inhospitable Batty Moss on its way into Cumbria. Opened in 1876, the 72 miles of line cost £47,500 a mile – an enormous sum at the time – and provided an entirely new route over the Pennines. During construction several shanty towns, complete with their own schools, hospitals and inns, were built along its course to house navvies from throughout Britain. With names such as Jericho and Salt Lake City nothing remains of them today, although in the bleak little churchyard of St Leonard's in Chapel-le-Dale there lie buried more than a hundred men who died from accidents and disease whilst building the line.

Left Looking towards the Ingleborough massif from near Stainforth in Upper Ribblesdale. Pot Scar, in the foreground, is one of many Carboniferous Limestone scars and 'pavements' shaped by the elements. The massif is dominated by the 2,373 feet high peak itself, topped by a 100 feet thick cap of hard wearing Millstone Grit which bears the foundations of prehistoric huts. Trees are few on the thin limestone soils, although a patch of the once widespread ash woodland is preserved on the slopes.

Looking down from Castlebergh Crag onto the old market town of Settle in Upper Ribblesdale. The Settle-Carlisle line divides the old part of the town in the foreground from the new part beyond. Prominent in the Market Square is the Olde Naked Man teashop, once an inn for travellers on the Leeds-Kendal road and still popular today. Also in the Square is the market cross, Town Hall, and the Shambles – where open-air business was once conducted. Apart from being involved with the tourist industry, the inhabitants of this workaday town find employment in the quarries of Upper Ribblesdale and in the many other small businesses which have developed in the area. In the distance is the green copper dome of Giggleswick School's chapel, founded by James Carr in the sixteenth century.

The natural amphitheatre of Malham Cove, one of the most spectacular limestone features of the Craven Fault system as it cuts across the landscape between Ingleton and Grassington. Since Victorian times the Cove, which now straddles the Pennine Way, has annually attracted thousands of visitors. The dry valley above the Cove once carried the outflow from Malham Tarn, one of Yorkshire's few natural lakes. The water has subsequently found its way underground through the many fissures in the limestone to re-emerge as the infant Aire to the south beyond Malham. The trickle that emerges from the base of the Cove in fact originates on Malham Moor to the west of the Tarn. Several times over the past few hundred years torrential rain has caused the Tarn outflow to once again descend the dry valley and create a brief 300 feet high waterfall over the lip of the Cove.

Right Large-scale lamb sales have occurred out in the open in Craven since the mid-eighteenth century and were once a regular and vital part of the local farming year. Sadly, the annual lamb sale held at Malham in August is the last of its kind, and is today more an opportunity to meet old friends and continue a tradition, although up to six hundred sheep may be sold on the day. In the past surplus 'mule' lambs (a cross between a Swaledale ewe and a Blue-Faced Leicester tup) were driven down off the pastures and auctioned to local farmers and visiting dealers from as far afield as Darlington and York. Still predominantly a local affair, the sale is continued by John and David Taylor, whose great-grandfather established the sale in its present form nearly 150 years ago.

Below Looking southwards towards Heights Scar and Calf Holes Cave, on the eastern edge of Malham Moor, and the gritstone heights of Cracoe and Rylstone Fells above Lintondale, a tributary valley of Upper Wharfedale. The line of the Mid-Craven Fault is clearly demonstrated in the foreground, the limestone scar and lush pasture on the left giving way to dark Gritstone moorland on the right. The top of the scar is believed to be the location of the lost Norse settlement of Hubbacove.

The view west along the length of Langstrothdale from the slopes of Buckden Pike in Upper Wharfedale. In the far distance is the whaleback outline of Whernside, at 2414 feet the highest of the Three Peaks. The fells of Upper Wharfedale between Buckden and the source of the Wharfe above Beckermonds ('the meeting of the becks') are some of Yorkshire's highest. In medieval times they made up the great deer and game reserve known as Langstroth ('long marsh') Chase, for which Buckden formed the main village and where the Forest Warden and his officials had their lodge. The wild scenery was popular with the Norse settlers, who farmed sheep here in the early tenth century and who must have found it reminiscent of their Scandinavian homelands.

The village of Kettlewell in Upper Wharfedale with Great Whernside (2310 feet) in the distance. Kettlewell was originally a Norse settlement, and its name is thought to mean 'bubbling spring', it being the place where several gushing becks converge. Since the late sixteenth century the village has been governed by its Trust Lords, a group of local freeholders who collected royalties from the nearby lead and coal mines, allocated grazing rights on common pastures, regulated peat cutting on the high tops and appointed game-keepers and shepherds. Radiating out from the village is a network of ancient packhorse routes such as the Top Mere Road (visible in the background), which climbs the flanks of Buckden Pike and crosses into Walden. Such 'green roads' were used to connect monasteries with their sheep runs or as drovers roads and packhorse ways, and are now popular routes for today's walkers.

Evening light bathes Horse Head Moor above the tiny hamlet of Halton Gill at the head of Littondale. Still one of the quietest and least spoilt of the Craven Dales, Littondale is a tributary valley of Upper Wharfedale, separated from the latter by the long moorland ridge of Old Cote Moor.

The village of Kilnsey in the lee of Kilnsey Crag, the most celebrated glacial feature in Upper Wharfedale. The Crag represents the final flourish of the Great Scar Limestone, stretching all the way from Ingleton before it vanishes beneath the younger Yoredales and Gritstones a little to the east of the Wharfe. The village was once owned by the monks of Fountains Abbey, and their sheep grange here was where the Malham Moor flocks were brought annually for clipping. They used the ancient 'green road' of Mastiles Lane to drive the sheep over the moors to Malham Fair. Today Kilnsey is the site of limestone quarrying, whilst the spring-fed lake has been developed as a trout farm and angling centre. The riverside pastures provide the venue for the annual Kilnsey Show, an attraction of which is the gruelling Crag Race.

Above Climbers attempting to conquer Kilnsey Crag which, although only 170 feet high, represents a considerable challenge because of its 40 foot overhang and was climbed as recently as 1957. The limestone formations of the Craven Dales provide a haven for climbers, especially around Malham Cove and Gordale Scar.

Below A lone hawthorn tree growing precariously on the limestone pavement of Hill Castles Scar above Conistone in Upper Wharfedale. Such pavements have been eroded post-glacially by water into blocks ('clints') separated by mini ravines ('grikes'). This so-called 'Karst Scenery' is a characteristic feature of the Great Scar Limestone between Ingleton and Grassington. Once raided for rockery and walling stone, it is now protected, the grikes sheltering many rare plants.

Above Looking northwards from Elbolton Hill across the town of Grassington in Upper Wharfedale towards the ridge of Great Whernside. Field systems belonging to Bronze and Iron Age settlements more than 2,000 years ago are still visible on the slopes above the village. The lower fields alongside the river were cultivated in the medieval period using strip lynchets. Gradually these early field systems were replaced by long walled fields carpeting the limestone terraces around the town as far as the open moorland grazings above. Today a thriving tourist centre which hosts a Dickensian Christmas fair, nineteenth century Grassington was the centre of the Upper Wharfedale lead mining field.

Left The attractive riverside village of Burnsall in Upper Wharfedale. The five-arched stone bridge is one of the sturdiest in the Dales, and was built originally by Sir William Craven in 1612 to replace a wooden predecessor. Craven hailed from nearby Appletreewick and was known as the 'Dick Whittington of the Dales' after he went to London and became Lord Mayor. In 1602 he endowed the Grammar School, a feature of many Dales villages and proof of how highly education was valued by these communities. Next to the school is the Church of St Wilfred where, in the seventh century, the saint planted his staff and preached. The church contains fragments of Anglian crosses and Norse hogs-back tombstones.

Below Since at least Elizabethan times celebrations have taken place at Burnsall in Wharfedale during August to celebrate the feast of St Wilfred. The culmination of Feast Week is the Saturday Feast and Sports, during which the gruelling Burnsall Fell Race is held. Dating from 1870, it involves a climb of 572 feet from the riverside to the fell top and the current record time stands at an exhausting 12 minutes 50 seconds.

Left A fresh fall of snow blankets the Miners' Bridge in Hebden Ghyll above Hebden village in Upper Wharfedale. The upper reaches of the ghyll border the Grassington Moor Lead Mining Field and at one time one of the country's first aerial ropeways carried lead ore down to the smelt mill at nearby Hole Bottom.

Left Painted by Turner and written about by Wordsworth, Bolton Priory was founded in 1154 on the banks of the Wharfe by Augustinian Canons who had moved here from nearby Embsay. Over the next four centuries they established one of Yorkshire's richest religious houses, their wealth coming from wool and lead mining. At the time of the Dissolution in 1540 the last prior, Richard Moon, was building the West Tower, which still remains unfinished. The Early English nave escaped destruction, and following its restoration by G. E. Street in 1880 became the parish church of the Blessed Virgin and St Cuthbert. The rest was sold to the Earl of Cumberland and much of the stone was re-used in building Bolton Hall, a shooting lodge now owned by the Duke of Devonshire, to whose ancestors the estate had passed by marriage.

Below The village of Wath, with Gouthwaite Reservoir in the background, looking north along Upper Nidderdale, the last and shortest of the main dales. In the distance is Little Whernside (1984 feet). Lying east of Wharfedale, Nidderdale's rugged character is dominated in its upper parts by a succession of great reservoirs. Gouthwaite was built in 1893 and, as well as sending some of its 1600 million gallons to distant Bradford, is today an important nature reserve.

The haunting geological phenomenon of Brimham Rocks near Pateley Bridge, formed 300 million years ago when a plateau of Millstone Grit was uncovered by glacial action. Subsequent erosion by wind and water has resulted in a series of fantastic shapes once thought to be the work of druids, hence names like Druid's Altar and Druid's Head. Successive generations of visitors have given names to individual rocks, such as the Dancing Bear, Devil's Anvil, the Sphinx and Indian's Turban.

The River Nidd winding its way along the deep wooded Magnesian Limestone gorge below the red-roofed town of Knaresborough. The town's attractions include the eighteenth century House in the Rock, the Petrifying Well, the sooth-saying Mother Shipton's Cave, as well as pleasure boats and tea houses, and it is no wonder that Yorkshire author Halliwell Sutcliffe described Knaresborough as 'like some pleasant foreigner come to settle in the North'. It was not always the case. The Castle was a temporary refuge for the knights responsible for the murder of Thomas á Becket, and Richard II was imprisoned in it. During the Civil War Cromwell starved out the Royalists who were holding it and, after his son had been killed, reduced it to ruins.

The unusual estate village of Ripley, just outside Harrogate, rebuilt in the style of a village in Alsace-Lorraine in the 1820s by Sir William Amcotts Ingilby of Ripley Castle. A mixture of Rhine *schloss* and French *chateaux*, much of the Castle dates from the 1870s, although at its core is a fortified manor house with a fifteenth century gatehouse. Continuing the French theme is the Town Hall, which was built in 1854 and bears the inscription 'Hotel de Ville'. The land had been given, originally, to Thomas Ingilby after he saved Edward III from a wild boar. During the Civil War Cromwell and his troops were billeted here after the Battle of Marston Moor, 15 miles to the east, and musket ball holes on the church wall bear witness to the execution of Royalist prisoners by the Roundheads during this time. The Castle gardens were laid out by 'Capability' Brown and it was Sir William who dammed Thornton Beck, a tributary of the Nidd, to form an ornamental lake.

Harrogate's Royal Pump Room, established in 1842 and containing the Old Sulphur Well, one of the eighty or so mineral springs discovered within a two mile radius of the town from as early as 1571. Rich in chalybeate, sulphur and iron, the many springs caused one seventeenth visitor to describe Harrogate as offering 'the best entertainment of any watering place in Britain at the least expense'. During the nineteenth century the newly prosperous industrial middle classes of the West Riding made the spa town a fashionable and prosperous watering place, Edward VII, amongst other dignitaries, spending the 'season' here. Consequently much of the town's architecture is solid, elegant Victorian and Edwardian interspersed with parks where visitors could promenade. The Royal Baths Assembly Room, opened in 1897, was once one of the world's largest hydrotherapy centres. Despite its closure in 1969, the legacy of grand hotels and well-maintained gardens that flourished when the town was fashionable has allowed Harrogate to prosper as a smart conference, festival and shopping centre. The Royal Pump Room, with its glass extension of 1913, now contains a museum illustrating the importance of spas to the early development of the town.

Montpellier Parade is typical of Harrogate's elegant streets dating from its Victorian and Edwardian heyday. The Parade's name stems from a French spa where many English families took up residence during the Napoleonic Wars. At the top end is the ever popular 'Betty's Cafe'. Serving the sort of cakes eaten in Continental spas such as Homburg and Marienbad, it still possesses its original art nouveau glass and iron canopy.

AIREDALE AND
MID-WHARFEDALE

"Where the gray flocks in ferny glens are feeding,
Where the wild wind blows on the mountain side."
Emily Brontë, *Stanzas*

THE River Aire rises south of Malham at Aire Head Springs in the heart of the limestone country of the Craven Highlands. By the time the Aire reaches Gargrave and the '*sheep town*' of Skipton it has left the limestone country far behind and enters the strikingly different Millstone Grit which dominates the landscape all the way into Derbyshire. Beyond Keighley the area is known as the South Pennines, a land of high windswept hills and moors broken by crags and empty expanses of peat bog and cotton grass. Grim and foreboding when inclement, but infinitely uplifting when clear, these 'lonely mountains' both inspired the writings of the Brontës of Haworth and contributed to their tragically early deaths.

South of Skipton, Mid-Airedale marks the transition from rural Ribblesdale and Mal-hamdale to the predominantly industrial landscapes of West Yorkshire. The isolated

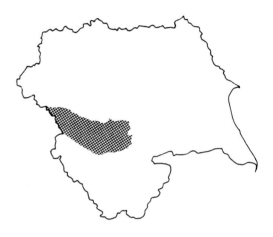

Previous page A collection of 'reed hooks', 'looming hooks', 'denters' and a 'twister's wire' from the Craven Museum in Skipton, together with an auctioneer's poster for the sale of the Good Intent Mill in 1844: relics from the cotton industry which flourished here after the opening of the High Mill in 1785. The three-storey Good Intent Mill was built in about 1822 in nearby Embsay by the Bradley family to produce cotton and worsted. It was successfully sold in 1844, but burnt down thirteen years later. The most celebrated manufacturer in the town was the firm of Dewhurst's who opened their first spinning mill in 1822. For over 160 years Dewhurst's produced their famous reels of sewing threads in the great mill, with its now sadly demolished brick chimney, near the railway station.

Left Narrow boats moored on the Springs Branch of the Leeds- Liverpool Canal at Skipton. Like other Pennine textile centres, the construction of the Canal and the opening of the Springs Branch in 1774 gave Skipton a westward outlet for its high quality worsted cloths.

farms and villages give way to market and mill towns: clog-making Silsden, Bingley with its staircase of locks on the Leeds-Liverpool Canal, and Shipley where Sir Titus Salt built his model industrial town of Saltaire in the 1850s. Water pouring off the wide hilltops down rocky cloughs and gills was used to power the many factories and textile mills in the valleys. Towns grew up in their shadow, but the brooding presence of the Pennine moors offered their inhabitants a chance to escape from the clatter of the mills and a way of life that the advent of the Industrial Revolution did little to improve.

The main industrial conurbations of Airedale are Leeds and Bradford. The birthplace of both J. B. Priestley and the composer Frederick Delius, Bradford has stood at the centre of the wool trade since the fourteenth century, generating sufficient wealth to allow later mill-owners to finance such extravagant Italianate buildings as the Wool Exchange and Town Hall. Leeds also owes its early prosperity to the medieval weaving and cloth trades. Similar to Sheffield in both size and population, the city has miraculously managed to retain a feeling of open space and natural woodland in its parks at Roundhay and Middleton, the Meanwood Valley and Temple Newsam. Barely two miles from the bustling city centre, the leafy 'village' of Headingley is home to Yorkshire cricket and one of the world's most famous grounds.

In direct contrast to Airedale, the middle and lower parts of the course of the Wharfe are still rural and relatively unsullied by industry. The elevated ridge of high country known as Rombaulds Moor – the watershed dividing industrial Airedale from Mid-Wharfedale – has long been an important route and contains a rich diversity of archaeological remains in the form of stone circles and the greatest concentration of prehistoric rock carvings in the country. Otley is a market town whose sixth and seventh century origins are indicated by a fine collection of early Christian crosses in the local church; whilst a little further downstream lies Harewood House, a jewel in Yorkshire's architectural and artistic crown.

The ruined engine house and chimney of the lead mine at Cononley, south of Skipton, marking the southern limit of the Craven Lead Mining Field which operated during the eighteenth and nineteenth centuries. Of the smelt mill at Cononley there are now no remains, but it was situated several hundred feet below in the narrow gill at the foot of the hill. The poisonous fumes contained a great deal of vapourised lead and were carried away by a flue which climbed to the discharge chimney on top of the hill. The inside of the flue was periodically scraped, often by young children – the removal of the lead condensed from the fumes considerably increasing the mine's total yield.

The remote Upper Worth Valley, west of Haworth, once carried a packhorse road through the heart of the Keighley and Haworth Moors from Bradford into Lancashire. The construction of the Watersheddles, Ponden and Lower Laithe Reservoirs depopulated the valley, although the village of Stanbury remains together with one of England's first Quaker burial grounds. Walled fields, the result of eighteenth century Enclosure Acts, climb the valley sides and are managed from hill farms whose cramped living quarters are typically extended into a long barn for livestock.

The Georgian parsonage at Haworth, a windswept hilltop village, and once the unlikely home of perhaps the most canonised literary family of the nineteenth century, the Brontës. Curate Patrick Brontë moved here, via Thornton in Bradford, from Cornwall in 1820, his wife Maria and elder daughters Elizabeth and Maria dying soon afterwards. Despite poverty, isolation and ill-health, the surrounding bleak moorland and harsh climate inspired the remaining daughters Charlotte (1816-1855), Emily (1818-1848) and Anne (1820-1849) to publish *Jane Eyre*, *Wuthering Heights* and *Agnes Grey* respectively in 1847 – a quite extraordinary achievement. The three sisters, together with their artist brother Branwell (1817-1848), all lived short, isolated lives in these grim surroundings. Emily died before her work was fully acknowledged, and Anne died in Scarborough in 1849 within six months of the publication of *The Tenant of Wildfell Hall*. *Jane Eyre* brought Charlotte considerable success, which she followed with *Shirley* (1849) and *Vilette* (1853). The following year she married her father's curate, dying only nine months later aged 39. Branwell drank himself to death in the nearby Black Bull Hotel. Their writings, however, have made them immortal and their home has become a place of pilgrimage.

The 4½ mile branch line known as the Keighley and Worth Valley Railway opened in 1867 to connect Keighley, Damens, Oakworth, Haworth and Oxenhope. Today lovingly restored steam engines carry visitors along the valley calling at period stations complete with tin advertisement boards and porters. Although this attention to historical detail from the heyday of steam travel has made it the star of such period films as 'The Railway Children', the line continues to be a reliable public transport service for the local community.

The Five Rise Locks at Bingley which, together with about ninety other locks, two tunnels and numerous aqueducts, carry the Leeds-Liverpool Canal to a height of 500 feet on its journey across the Pennines. Construction of the 127 mile long trans-Pennine canal, the longest in Britain, was authorised by Act of Parliament in 1770 with John Longbottom of Halifax as engineer and was finished in 1816 at a final cost of £824,000. The route posed a succession of difficulties, one of which was the steep gradient at Bingley, where the five locks lift the canal bed 60 feet over a distance of 300 feet. Once completed, the canal provided a through route from Liverpool to West Yorkshire and, via the Aire and Calder Navigation, to the Humber and Hull, as well as a more local service for the towns on its route. Today it is enjoyed by narrow boats, pleasure cruisers and towpath walkers.

Above The model town of Saltaire, the first of its kind in England, established by entrepreneur and philanthropist Sir Titus Salt alongside the Leeds-Liverpool Canal in the Aire Valley. In 1850 Salt abandoned his Bradford mills and moved his workforce to what was then open country at Shipley. He opened Europe's largest mill – christened 'The Palace of Industry' – in 1853, producing 30,000 yards of alpaca a day, a silky material woven from llama wool. His employees lived in neat rows of sandstone terraces and were provided with schools, almshouses, church (left), library, laundry and park; but he forbade pubs and pawnshops, being a devout Congregationalist. Although the mill closed when merino wool replaced alpaca the area has subsequently been redeveloped to include a gallery featuring artists such as Bradford-born David Hockney.

Right A detail of the entrance to the Wool Exchange in Bradford, built in 1869 in a flamboyant Venetian-Flemish Gothic style where, on market days, it was said 'there was not a single type of wool or hair for which a buyer could not be found'. Flanking the entrance are statues of Bishop Blaize, patron saint of wool combers, and Edward III, who reversed the declining wool trade in the fourteenth century. Victorian Bradford led the world's woollen trade, its steep streets lined with splendid commercial and civic buildings which were a far cry from the small town which existed here in the Middle Ages. With the arrival of the turnpikes, the Leeds-Liverpool Canal, and steam power the population of 1,600 in 1810 grew to 103,768 in 1851 as workers poured in to man the new mills. Despite catastrophic decline there is still a wool industry in what remains Yorkshire's grandest Victorian city.

The celebrated Bradford-born author and playright J.B. Priestley (1894-1984) – immortalised in bronze – surveys his beloved city from his plinth opposite the gleaming domes of the 1800 seat Alhambra Theatre, a superb Edwardian pleasure palace opened as a music hall in 1914 and now restored to its former glory. The large dome on the right belongs to the Odeon Cinema, which opened in 1930 with seats for more than 3,000 people. Completing the city's entertainment quarter is the nearby National Museum of Photography, Film and Television, home of IMAX, Britain's largest cinema screen.

The 240 feet high Italianate Campanile chimney of the vast Lister's Mill towers over Oak Lane at Manningham, Bradford, round the top of which its owner, Samuel Cunliffe Lister, claimed a horse and carriage could be driven. It opened in the 1870s to manufacture silk velvets and covered 16 acres, had a 350 yard long frontage and 7,000 employees, making it the world's largest factory at the time. Although textiles are still produced in Bradford the city can no longer lay claim to its name 'Worstedopolis' and the remaining mills are being redeveloped. Oak Lane, in the foreground, now hosts a colourful array of Pakistani general stores, run by some of Bradford's new generation of merchants.

A view of the centre of Leeds from Holbeck Cemetery, Beeston. Visible on the skyline is the white tower of the Parkinson Building of the University of Leeds, whilst on the right are both the domed clock tower of the Town Hall and the Civic Centre. By the fifteenth century the ancient village of 'Loidis' had grown into a major cloth manufacturing town that attracted clothiers to its markets and exported goods down the River Aire. In 1770 the population was about 16,000, but by 1850, when the railway and the Leeds-Liverpool Canal had both arrived, it had grown to 150,000. Victorian Leeds could boast an enviably diverse array of enterprises, including the mass-production of ready to wear clothing at Hepworth's and Burton's, railway locomotives from Murray and Blenkinsop, Fowler's traction engines, the Yorkshire Penny Bank and the very first Penny Bazaar – run by Messrs Marks and Spencer.

The monument on the right is to Thomas Beecroft, who in 1851 at the age of 19 invented what many regard as the world's first practical sewing machine.

The great commercial development of Leeds during the late Victorian period is well-represented by the sumptuous decoration of the city's County Arcade. Possibly the most flamboyant of its type in the country, and built by theatre architect Frank Matcham (1854-1920), designer of the Blackpool Tower Ballroom, it is a heady cocktail of marble, glass, cast iron and locally made faience. Recently restored as part of the Victoria Quarter, it is one of several arcades built by the Leeds Estate Company to profitably connect already established streets and markets.

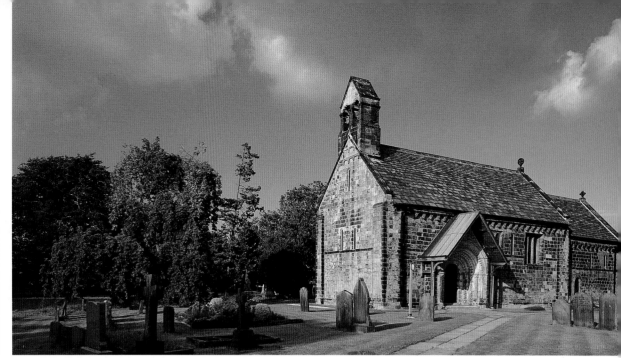

Above A view of the Egyptian-style façade of James Marshall's Temple Mill, built in 1838-43 in the Holbeck area of Leeds. Revolutionary for its time, this linen mill was unlike the usual 'dark satanic mills' in that it was an open and airy single-storey building lit by skylights and temperature controlled. The exterior was designed by Durham architect-cum-Egyptologist Joseph Bonomi, who was responsible for many of the fine Italianate buildings in Leeds.

Above right The Church of St John the Baptist at Adel, a village north of Leeds, is one of England's finest Norman churches, remaining virtually unaltered since its construction in about 1140. The elaborately carved south doorway is today protected by a porch, and the door itself is furnished with a brass sanctuary knocker. It depicts a tiny man in the jaws of a monster and is thought to represent the power of the church in saving mankind from the clutches of evil.

Right Brick-built Temple Newsam, on the outskirts of Leeds, which has been dubbed the 'Hampton Court of the North' although its style is Jacobean rather than Tudor, having been rebuilt in about 1630. Standing on land which once belonged to the Knights Templar – hence its name – the original building was the birthplace in 1545 of Henry, Lord Darnley, second husband of Mary Queen of Scots and father of James I. In 1622 the house was bought by wealthy courtier Sir Arthur Ingram (d.1642) whose family held and extended it until 1922 when it passed to the City of Leeds, who now maintain it as a museum. The 900 acres in which it stands is Europe's largest urban park.

Right The town of Ilkley in mid-Wharfedale. It has a long history that dates from Iron Age times, whilst its churchyard contains the foundations of a Roman fort and three fine Anglian crosses. During the eighteenth and nineteenth centuries it became an elegant spa town whose hotels offered health-giving waters, fresh air and alpine scenery. In the foreground is the edge of Ilkley Moor, a part of Rombaulds Moor which forms the watershed between Airedale and Wharfedale, famous for Yorkshire's national anthem, 'On Ilkla' Moor baht 'at', said to have been written in 1886 when a Halifax church choir had a summer picnic on the Moor.

Below The statue of Thomas Chippendale in Otley, the medieval market town where the great cabinet-maker was born in 1718. Much of his work can be seen in the county, notably at Harewood House and Nostell Priory.

Below right One of the reservoirs in the Washburn Valley, which stretches from the River Wharfe near Otley northwards to the moorland source of the River Washburn high on Pockstones Moor near Greenhow Hill. On the skyline are the eye-catching white 'golf balls' of the Menwith Hill Satellite Communications Station, a surrealistic addition to an otherwise pastoral landscape.

The south front of Harewood House, built in the local honey-coloured sandstone, between Leeds and Harrogate. Work on the estate began in the twelfth century with the now ruined Harewood Castle, as well as nearby Gawthorp Hall. Both passed through the hands of several families until the entire estate was bought in 1739 by wealthy Yorkshireman Henry Lascelles, who had made a fortune in ribbons, sugar and the East India Company. It was his son Edwin who decided to build anew, commissioning John Carr of York to begin construction of the present Palladian house with its side pavilions in 1759. Robert Adam added the beautiful neo-Classical interior in the late 1760s, Chippendale provided the furniture, and the paintings include works by Gainsborough and Reynolds. At the same time the old village of Harewood was rebuilt outside the park, itself laid out by Capability Brown. With the Earl of Harewood, a cousin of the Queen, still in residence, the house and its celebrated Bird Garden remain a firm favourite with visitors.

The photograph on the left shows a line-up of vintage and scale-model traction engines at the annual Harewood Steam Rally in the grounds of Harewood House.

A fisherman in the peaceful, deep-flowing River Wharfe, in sight of the fine bridge of 1770 built to connect the parishes of Boston Spa and Thorp Arch. Boston Spa has pleasant Georgian houses and a Royal Hotel as befits a one-time spa town established after a labourer discovered a spring near the river in 1744. Originally the spring was reached by ferry from Thorp Arch on the opposite bank.

The magnificent Gothic Gascoigne Almshouses outside the eighteenth century coaching town of Aberford on the old Great North Road near Tadcaster. They were erected in 1844 by Mary and Elizabeth Gascoigne of nearby Parlington Hall in memory of their father and two brothers, all of whom died within a year of each other. Designed by George Fowler Jones of York when only 26 years old, the building once housed eight elderly former tenants of the family estate.

CALDERDALE AND
THE COLNE VALLEY

CALDERDALE AND THE COLNE VALLEY

' . . . [there is not] anything more beautiful than the steep
mountains clothed with wood to the top, and washed
at the bottom by a clear winding stream.'

So wrote John Wesley, the eighteenth century founder of Methodism, after one of his many visits to Calderdale, where the stark landscape bred a tough and independent people drawn naturally towards Non-Conformity. For like Airedale to the north, Calderdale is typical of the South Pennines, being carved out of the dark Millstone Grit which stretches from Skipton to the Peak District.

The Yorkshire Calder rises ignominiously to the west of Todmorden, close to the Lancashire border where packhorse ways for the transporting of wool, cotton and salt have criss-crossed the hills since before the Middle Ages. For most of its course along the steep-sided Calder Valley the river jostles for space beside road, railway and canal, weaving its way between the dozens of mills and factories which so characterise this part of Yorkshire. Its tributaries rise high on desolate moorland whose bleakness has been reduced by the construction of reservoirs at the headwaters of all the larger becks. Before these

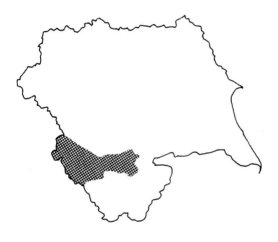

Previous page A typical Pennine 'millscape' near Slaithwaite in the Colne Valley, typified by the tangle of textile factories, chimneys, railway, road and canal lining the valley floor. The mill on the right dwarfs the house in front with its row of 'weavers' windows' where hand-looms were once worked.

Left Widdop Reservoir, which forms part of the upper reaches of Graining Water below the wild expanse of Widdop Moor on the high border country between West Yorkshire and Lancashire's Forest of Trawden. Between Haworth to the north and Todmorden to the south virtually every valley on this high moorland has been dammed to create reservoirs. Alcomden and Graining Waters combine to form Hebden Water which flows via Hardcastle Crags to meet the Yorkshire Calder at Hebden Bridge.

Above A close-up of the facade of the Town Hall at Todmorden, a mill town on the banks of the youthful Calder close to the Lancashire border. Commissioned in 1870 by the Fieldens, a family of local cotton magnates, this grand Classical building has a frieze depicting local industries – namely bales of cotton and wool – and a central plinth on which sit two embracing women. Beneath them are inscribed the words 'Yorkshire and Lancashire', such images and words reflecting the fact that Todmorden once lay on the original county boundary.

Above right The curious paved road which crosses the exposed Blackstone Edge at Rishworth Moor high on the Yorkshire-Lancashire border. The traveller Celia Fiennes wrote in her *Journeys* in 1698 that it was 'noted all over England for a dismal high precipice . . . these hills stagnate the air and hold mist and rain almost perpetually'. In 1725 Daniel Defoe claimed to have been caught in a blizzard here in August! Numerous coins found in the area suggest this was a Roman road connecting Manchester with Ilkley, although it may have been part of a medieval packhorse way down the Ryburn Valley.

tributaries converge and enter the main valley, each enjoys a brief period of youth, cutting its way through precipitous gills and producing the type of grand alpine scenery that caused the ever-romantic Victorians to describe Hardcastle Crags as a 'Little Switzerland'.

Of Norman origins, Halifax also gained its importance from the textile trade, its early merchants resorting to the introduction of the once notorious gibbet to deter thieves from stealing cloth pieces left out to dry. As with so many of West Yorkshire's congested and cramped mill towns, the recreation offered by the empty hills with their miles of lanes and footpaths is always at hand: places such as Rishworth Moor and the forbidding Blackstone Edge have been popular walking country for generations of ramblers. Dewsbury, in the Spen Valley, was a centre of the rag and heavy woollen trade and is surrounded by a populous area of towns and villages such as Batley, Cleckheaton, Liversedge and Heckmondwike – which today are straight-jacketed by motorways.

Despite the many coal workings around Wakefield, the Magnesian Limestone belt produces a countryside rich in rolling woodlands and parks. Nostell Priory, Ackworth and Bretton Park occupy this unexpectedly quiet corner of Yorkshire and provide a welcome respite from industrialisation before the Calder joins the Aire near Castleford.

The Colne and the Holme Valleys are also highly industrialised, but display quite different personalities. Like Calderdale, the Colne Valley is dominated by river, road, railway and canal, a fact brought home most clearly at Marsden where both the latter disappear into separate tunnels beneath the Pennines on their journey west, while the road climbs laboriously up over the moors. Downstream from Marsden, much of the valley is a tangle of textile mills and chimneys, producing an industrial backdrop characteristic of this part of Yorkshire. The Holme Valley is, by contrast, rather more open with a slightly wilder aspect than the Colne. From the heights of Holme Moss, the view to the north and east looks out over the county's heartland, whilst to the south there is only the aptly-named Black Peak – mile after mile of moorland and peat bog.

The Pennine village of Heptonstall, perched high above the junction of the Calder Valley and Hebden Water. The village was a prosperous medieval hand-weaving centre, and its Cloth Hall was the first in the Pennines where cloth was bought and sold. With the coming of mechanisation business moved down to the mills of Hebden Bridge in the valley below. Beside the Victorian church tower are the graves of David Hartley, executed in 1770 for clipping sovereigns, and American poetess Sylvia Plath (1932-1963). Also of interest is John Wesley's Methodist chapel, the oldest in continuous use. In the distance, on the edge of a spur of the gritstone moors, is the Stoodley Pike obelisk erected by public subscription to commemorate the surrender of Paris during the Napoleonic Wars in 1814.

Crimsworth Beck, a tributary of the Calder, running off Cock Hill Moor down the wooded Crimsworth Dean into Hardcastle Crags. The beck is crossed by Lumb Bridge, one of numerous packhorse bridges which carried the many tracks and paved 'causeys' across the South Pennines. During the seventeenth and eighteenth centuries this track was known as the Limers' Way, and was used to transport limestone from Wycoller in Lancashire over to Halifax.

Above Clog making at Frank Walkley's Mill, Hawksclough, on the River Calder near Hebden Bridge. Owned originally by John Maude & Son in 1870, clogging at Hawksclough reached its peak in the 1940s when the workforce was eighty strong and the sound of clogs on cobbles was still commonplace throughout the north of England. Today, although run on a smaller scale, clogs continue to be made for steel and agricultural workers and the fashion trade, as well as for export (even to Holland). Seasoned German beech, which once arrived by canal, is shaped into soles to which irons are nailed and leather uppers attached, producing the most hard-wearing footwear available.

Above Terraced workers' housing lining the valley sides at Hebden Bridge, a medieval crossing place over Hebden Water. The town is almost entirely the product of the eighteenth century Industrial Revolution when people moved down from the hills into the narrow valleys to be close to the new automated textile mills, dye works and iron foundries. Despite industrial decline Hebden Bridge is today a surprisingly thriving tourist centre for the South Pennines.

Right The towing of the rushcart during the annual Rush Bearing at Sowerby Bridge. The custom of rushbearing dates back several centuries to a time when rushes provided winter floor covering in churches. Each year the old rushes were exchanged for freshly harvested replacements, brought to the village on a specially made cart. In Cheshire, Lancashire, parts of Cumbria and West Yorkshire a lively festival developed around the procession of the rushcart and in 1977 the custom was revived as a community event in Sowerby Bridge. Over two days the procession winds its way from where the rushes are gathered up on the moor, through Sowerby Bridge and over the hills around the Ryburn Valley leaving, at each church, a token bundle of rushes. The Rush Cart is accompanied by teams of Morris men, clog dancers, musicians and Mummers and the journey is interrupted by frequent pauses to sample the inns along the way.

Above The Bradshaw Mummers of Halifax dressed to perform the story of Lord Nelson at the Battle of Trafalgar. Mumming Plays are traditionally performed at Christmas, the New Year or Easter, and, like many of Yorkshire's other ancient seasonal rituals – notably the Pace Egg Plays, Sword Dances and the Plough Stotts – symbolise the death of the old year and winter and the rebirth of the new with spring. Meaning either 'mask' or 'to act dumb', mummers wear hats and blacken their faces since recognition of the players was thought to break the luck their performance was believed to bring.

Left Halifax, one of Yorkshire's oldest towns, seen from Beacon Hill. Halifax has been an important textile centre since the thirteenth century, creating the wealth which produced the magnificent Gothic parish church of St John in the foreground. Beyond the church is the matchless Georgian Piece Hall of 1775 where weavers sold their 'pieces' of cloth to visiting merchants. Beyond are the equally impressive offices of the Halifax Building Society, built in the 1970s. The world's largest building society since 1927, its present premises are a far cry from the room above a shop in the Old Market where it was founded in 1853. In the far distance, on one of the hills which surround the town, can be seen the 253 feet high Wainhouse Tower, built originally as a dyeworks chimney but completed as a folly observatory.

Above A group of young maypole dancers taking part in the annual May weekend celebrations at Gawthorpe, between Dewsbury and Wakefield. An earlier Gawthorpe maypole was nearly toppled by the men of neighbouring Chickenley in 1850, and one man was killed in the fight that followed.

Above right The Cathedral of All Saints at Wakefield, once the county town of the old West Riding, reflected in the modern glass of the award winning Ridings Shopping Centre. Wakefield's Georgian and Regency architecture reflects its administrative importance, although it has also been an important weaving, dyeing and mining centre. The Cathedral, completed in 1329, was built over Saxon and Norman remains, and its 247 feet spire is the tallest in West Yorkshire. Wakefield's continued prosperity is assured by its position at the junction of the M1 and M62 motorways.

Right The east front of the Palladian mansion of Nostell Priory at Wragby, near Wakefield. It stands on the site of an Augustinian priory founded in the early twelfth century. After the Dissolution the estate was sold to the Winns, a family of London merchants. In 1729 the fourth Baronet, Sir Rowland Winn, returned from the Grand Tour of Europe and began work on an Italian-style mansion under the supervision of the brilliant architect James Paine, then only nineteen years old. Under the fifth Baronet, Paine's Rococo interiors were completed by Robert Adam, who also added the north wing (right). Thomas Chippendale of Otley furnished the entire house, right down to the kitchen chopping block and the furniture for a doll's house. Today the house is the home of Lord and Lady St Oswald.

The market place at Pontefract with its Buttercross and the unusual tower of the parish church of St Giles. The Buttercross was erected in 1734 by the widow of Solomon Dupier, a member of Gibraltar's Spanish garrison who, through betrayal, assisted the Anglo-Dutch invasion of the rock in 1704. Pontefract, Shakespeare's 'Pomfret', is chiefly known for liquorice and its medieval Castle – the last major Royalist stronghold in the Civil War to fall to Cromwell. Only a fragment of the tower and graffiti scratched by prisoners in the dungeons survive. The nearby ruins of All Saints Church, which was in the line of fire, still clearly show the scars left by Cromwell's cannon.

The Huddersfield Narrow Canal at Marsden in the Colne Valley where it enters the Standedge Tunnel on its way under the Pennines to Greater Manchester. At 3 miles and 176 yards the tunnel is the longest and highest in Britain, and accounted for much of the £400,000 which the 20 mile long canal cost. Begun in 1794 to connect Manchester with Hull and not opened until 1811, it gave rise to a lament from investors: 'This vile canal as I'm a sinner, It steals alike my cash and dinner.' It was bought in 1844 when canal receipts were flagging and used to assist in the construction of the adjacent railway tunnels, to which the canal was joined by interconnecting shafts. The canal tunnel finally closed in 1942, although there are now plans to renovate and reopen it.

Above A panorama of Huddersfield from Castle Hill, Almondbury. The town was an important centre of the domestic weaving trade, with a market dating from 1672. In 1776 Sir Joshua Ramsden, the Lord of the Manor, built a Cloth Hall where 'pieces' were bought and sold. Industrial expansion in the eighteenth and nineteenth centuries made the town one of West Yorkshire's great textile centres, famous for its worsted cloths. Different grades were used for a variety of goods, including suits, stockings and carpets. The town was also noted for dyeing and wholesale tailoring. As the Ramsdens owned much of the town centre it was they who encouraged canals and rail links and the construction of handsome warehouses around the station. To the left, on higher ground are extensive Victorian and Edwardian suburbs, such as Lindley and Edgerton. In 1920 the Corporation bought the town, hence it being known as 'the town that bought itself'.

Right The spectacular Classical façade of Hudderfield's railway station, described by Sir John Betjeman as the 'most splendid station façade in England'. Designed by York architect J.P. Pritchett the Elder in 1847-48, its façade is 416 feet long and dominated by a central columned porch worthy of a Roman temple. The flanking wings end in similar porticos bearing the arms of the Lancashire & Yorkshire Railway and the Huddersfield and Manchester Railway & Canal Company. That the two should combine to produce so grand a building, in what was at the time only a modest settlement, seems curious. In fact both companies were competing for the line's contract, eventually deciding to share it; an agreement still celebrated in the building itself.

The Jubilee Tower on Castle Hill at Almondbury, south of Huddersfield, erected in 1899 for Queen Victoria's Diamond Jubilee. The hill, which commands impressive views along the Colne and Holme Valleys, has yielded evidence of occupation since about 2,000 BC. During the Iron Age and Romano-British period the Brigantes had a hill-fort here and it was long thought to be the site of the 'capital' of the Celtic Queen Cartimandua, now considered to be situated at Aldborough (*Isurium Brigantium*) near Boroughbridge. The Normans built a fortress on the hill, which was used as a hunting lodge before its demolition in the fourteenth century. The beacon in the foreground is thought to stand on the site of one lit to warn of the approaching Spanish Armada.

A skilled mill worker watching over a magnificent ninety-year old Huddersfield-built Spinning Mule in the Holme Spinning Co.'s Fearnley Mill at Bradley, on the outskirts of Huddersfield. Situated in a fine old multi-storey mill, built of dark gritstone blackened by the smoke of industrial West Yorkshire, the Holme Spinning Co. prides itself on following traditional methods of woollen yarn manufacture. Much of their yarn is made by recycling stocking wool which is shredded, combed, carded and transformed into raw thread. To provide strength, a precisely measured amount of twist is put into it by the intricate movements of the Spinning Mule. Sights such as this would have been commonplace fifty years ago when virtually everybody in the area worked 'in t'mill'.

Looking north-east along the Holme Valley from Holme Moss, a wild area of Pennine moorland which divides West Yorkshire from the High Peak of Derbyshire. Yateholme Reservoir, on the right, is one of several in these wet highlands supplying, amongst other places, the town of Holmfirth in the middle distance. On the far horizon, towards the right, can be seen the Emley Moor television mast and steam rising from power stations at the southern end of the Vale of York.

Terraces alongside Holme Beck, running through the old wool town of Holmfirth. It is a closely packed community of steep hills, cobbled streets and a skyline of stepped roofs broken up by its two churches and town hall. Squeezed into a deep valley and surrounded by bleak moors, Holmfirth has experienced three great floods in its history. But it owes its more recent fame, and its many visitors, to providing the setting for the television series 'Last of the Summer Wine'.

THE BOROUGHS OF
SOUTH YORKSHIRE

*'All the way along, from Leeds to Sheffield,
it is coal and iron, and iron and coal.'*
William Cobbett, *Rural Rides*, 1830

ORIGINALLY a part of the vast West Riding, what is now South Yorkshire was a creation of the 1974 boundary changes. Although sadly overlooked in many books on Yorkshire, it would be wrong to turn one's back on an area so much an essential part of the county in favour of the more picturesque moors and dales. This is plain-speaking, down-to-earth Yorkshire, the Yorkshire of coal and steel, of 'where there's muck there's brass'.

Its main river is the Don, which runs for seventy miles from the gritstone moors straddling the border between Yorkshire and the Derbyshire Peak District to where it ends in a confusion of canals and cuts at Rawcliffe Bridge, not far from Goole. The landscape through which it flows is a surprising patchwork of open moors, urban sprawl, woodland and farmsteads in abrupt succession. Although South Yorkshire as a whole lacks any geographical unity, it may be conveniently considered in terms of its four Metropolitan Districts of Sheffield, Rotherham, Barnsley and Doncaster.

Set on seven hills, like Rome, Sheffield developed from a small settlement in a river valley to become the county's largest city. A true child of the Industrial Revolution, the free availability of iron, charcoal, clay and coal underwrote the city's prosperity. The same raw materials also fostered the invention of crucible steel and Sheffield plate, putting Sheffield

Previous page Sheffield cutler Stan Shaw still working at his bench, despite the virtual extinction of such individual craftsmanship in Sheffield and a flood of cheap, mass-produced imports. His workshop is scarcely different from those of the nineteenth century, when master cutlers, known as 'Little Mesters', worked alone at rented spaces in factories, selling their work on at the end of each week. All the tools and materials required for the forty or so processes necessary to produce high quality knives are visible, most of them fashioned by Stan himself to his own personal specifications – vice, hammers, files, drills, polishing wheels, steel, brass, and some horn.

Left Damflask Reservoir, seen from the ancient Castle Hill in High Bradfield, a mere five or six miles from the busy centre of Sheffield. It lies in the valley of the River Loxley which, together with the Rivelin and the Ewden, form part of a beautiful and underrated area of woodland, moorland and gritstone crags equal to anything in the nearby Peak District National Park.

Above The Grenoside Sword Dancers in the Old Red Lion at Grenoside, just outside Sheffield. Usually performed on Boxing Day, sword dancing seems to be a Yorkshire version of the Morris Dance.

Above right Sheffield's restored Lyceum Theatre (right) is now the focal point of the city's theatre district. It was built in the 1890s by W.G.R. Sprague, and the interior is a typically glorious riot of Rococo plasterwork. The Crucible Theatre (left) opened in 1971 and is one of Britain's most modern theatres, with two auditoria, the largest of which seats a thousand people. The Crucible is known to snooker fans as the venue for the World Championship.

Below Sheffield's Botanical Gardens opened in 1836 on 20 acres and gradually established themselves as a place where visitors could enjoy Joseph Paxton's trio of glass pavilions, based on the Crystal Palace. The plantings include rock, woodland and heather gardens together with extensive lawns, mature trees and flower beds.

cutlery on tables the world over. The city's expansion had a price. The nineteenth century writer John Ruskin described it as a 'dark picture in a golden frame', blackened like so many Yorkshire towns by centuries of chimney smoke. With the demise of heavy industry and the imposition of clean air laws, Sheffield is now in the process of reinventing itself as a centre for tourism, light industry and the production of special steels.

Rotherham is a microcosm of Yorkshire's long history, with each wave of invaders passing on something to the next. A Roman fort was succeeded by a Saxon church. After the Norman Conquest William I gave the manor to his half-brother. And as with history, so also with Rotherham's industrial legacy. Coal mines were opened, followed by iron, steel and brass foundries. To the south-east, close to the Nottinghamshire border, a surprisingly wooded and peaceful area shelters the ruins of Roche Abbey and small market towns such as Tickhill.

Barnsley – its name betraying its origins as a woodland clearing – lies in the broad valley of the River Dearne, which joins the Don between Mexborough and Conisbrough. Again, one landscape shades imperceptibly into the next, but the abiding features are the dozens of grassed-over slag heaps that stand like domed memorials to the once great Yorkshire Coalfield. Barnsley's own long history of deep mining began with surface pickings in the fifteenth century. The gradual closure of the mines has allowed the many attractive villages in the area, such as Denby Dale and Cawthorne, to wash off the centuries of grime and show themselves in their true colours.

Doncaster was founded by the Romans as an important hub on their road network, and in some ways the town's position and transport have marched hand in hand through its history. By the eighteenth century it was a coaching stop on the Great North Road; by the end of the nineteenth a railway junction famous for its carriage works and repair sheds. All but a handful of the neighbouring coal mines – kept viable by reinvestment – have fallen victim to cheap imports and alternative fuels.

To the north-east lies Thorne Waste, or Moors, a vast marshy fenland which stretches from the medieval hunting preserve of Hatfield Chase as far north as Goole and east into Lincolnshire. During the reign of Charles I the Dutch engineer Vermuyden drained the Moors and transformed the last few miles of the Don into a canal, known to this day as the 'Dutch River'. Travelling through this flat landscape is an odd experience, for it is unique to Yorkshire, and unlike anywhere else in the county.

The former industrial heartland of Sheffield's East End spread out across the lower Don Valley. In the foreground is the twin-decked Tinsley Viaduct carrying the M1 north and south, beyond which is the green dome of the huge Meadowhall Shopping Centre. An array of colourful sports facilities, offices and shopping malls are gradually replacing the old steelworks and factories: a far cry from Daniel Defoe's impression of Sheffield in the 1720s, '. . .the streets narrow, and the houses dark and black occasioned by the continued smoke of the forges, which are always at work. . .'

Pouring molten steel into a mould at the Davy Roll Company in Sheffield's East End. This part of the Don Valley was once ablaze with furnaces producing everything from cutlery to huge steel plates for the hulls of Dreadnought battleships. Despite the industry's overall decline, Sheffield has retained its importance as a world centre for special steels. The Davy Roll Company, together with its Gateshead operation, produces 18,000 tonnes of high grade steel a year.

Above The spectacular east front of Wentworth Woodhouse which, at 606 feet, is the longest country house in Europe. Hidden in woodland between the Don and Dearne rivers, the core of the house was built in 1630 by Thomas Wentworth (1593-1641), Earl of Strafford and ill-fated Chief Minister to Charles I. After his execution in the Tower the estate passed, via the second Earl and his nephew, to the latter's son Thomas Watson-Wentworth (1693-1750), an aspiring Whig politician eager to impress Walpole and his voters, who added the Baroque West Range. As soon as the work was complete, and by now Earl Malton, he began constructing the East Range in the then fashionable Palladian style. This created today's unusual back-to-back country house, each range facing different directions and without direct access. After standing firm against the Scots at Culloden the Earl was made First Marquis of Rockingham (1746) after which the estate passed, in 1750, to Charles Watson-Wentworth, 2nd Marquis of Rockingham (1730-1782), twice Prime Minister. Following his death the Wentworth name died out and the house passed to the Fitzwilliam family. After a spell as a college the house is once again in private hands and is undergoing a welcome programme of restoration.

Above Rotherham's Bridge Chapel of All Saints over the River Don, and its more elaborate counterpart over the Calder in Wakefield, are two of the only four bridge chapels remaining in England. Known as Chantry Chapels, from the Old French *chanterie*, they were places where masses were sung for their founders, patrons and grateful laity. Funds were collected from travellers for the upkeep of the bridge in return for prayers for their safety. Rotherham's chapel was founded in 1483 by Thomas Rotherham, later Archbishop of York. It was subsequently used as an almshouse in the sixteenth century, the town prison in 1779, a newsagent's and tobacconist's in 1888 and re-dedicated in 1924 by the Bishop of Sheffield.

The Market Place at Tickhill, occupied by the Buttercross erected by the then vicar, Christopher Alderson, in 1777 and restored by his granddaughter in 1898. On the left is the village pump and on the right an old road sign proclaiming 'TICKHILL YORKS W.R.', reflecting the fact that South Yorkshire was once a part of the West Riding. In 1178 Henry II built a stone keep here on the 75 feet 'Tica's hill', making it one of the most important castles in Northern England and the centre of the vast Honour of Tickhill. Although it was slighted by the Parliamentarians in the Civil War the curtain wall survives. By the fourteenth century medieval Tickhill had become the second largest market town in South Yorkshire, a status it has long since surrendered.

The ruined east end of the Abbey of St Mary of Roche. The Abbey was founded in 1147 by the Cistercians, its name reflecting the rocky Limestone crags surrounding the secluded valley in which it stands, and by the end of the twelfth century was occupied by some 80 monks and lay brothers. The Abbey was surrendered to the Crown in 1538, by which time only the abbot and 18 monks remained, and much of its masonry was immediately robbed by locals. The ruins later formed the centrepiece of a landscape created in 1776 by 'Capability' Brown for nearby Sandbeck Park.

Above The unmistakeable profile of the old pit-head winding gear at Maltby Colliery near Rotherham. Maltby opened in 1908 and is now one of less than ten deep mines remaining in the South Yorkshire coalfield. In the 1980s British Coal chose to invest heavily in Maltby, building a revolutionary new concrete winding tower over the Parkgate seam 3,251 feet below. The new winding machinery in the tower takes a mere two minutes to raise 160 miners in a huge triple-decker lift from the coal face. It is expected to produce in excess of five million tonnes of coal a year, guaranteeing the colliery's survival until well into the 21st century. The coal measures along the eastern flanks of the Pennines had been mined locally for centuries, but it was not until the Industrial Revolution of the mid-eighteenth century that output dramatically increased to meet the demands of iron smelting and the firing of steam engines. Mining came to dominate the landscape, and its way of life, and by the beginning of the twentieth century the South Yorkshire coalfield was responsible for a quarter of all the coal mined in Great Britain. Today most of the mines have shut in the face of imports and alternative fuels, their equipment has been dismantled and the slag-heaps landscaped.

Top right A miner clocking off at Maltby Colliery after working a seven hour shift at the coal face.

Right The monument in All Saints churchyard at Silkstone commemorating the 26 children drowned at the Huskar Pit in 1838. The boys and girls, several under the age of ten, were caught climbing out of a ventilation shaft during a rainstorm, the main lift having failed. The young Queen Victoria sent her condolences, and an Act of 1842 finally prohibited boys under ten and females from working underground. The human price of coal mining has always been tragically high, and the churchyards of South Yorkshire are littered with epitaphs to its victims.

Above '...there are few more beautiful or striking scenes in England than are presented by the vicinity of this ancient fortress; the soft and gentle River Don sweeps through an amphitheatre, in which cultivation is richly blended with woodland, and on a mount ascending from the river rises this ancient edifice...'. So wrote Sir Walter Scott of Conisbrough Castle, its spectacular cylindrical Norman keep providing the inspiration for 'Rotherwood' in his novel *Ivanhoe*. It began life as a wooden palisade built by William de Warenne, granted the land by William I in recognition of the part he played in the Norman Conquest of England. Hamelin Plantagenet erected the keep in 1180, and in 1994 English Heritage painstakingly reconstructed its original wooden floors and roof to protect the near-perfect fabric from the further ravages of the weather and pollution.

Left Barnsley's civic pride reflected in this old fashioned wrought iron bandstand in Locke Park. The Park's 46 acres were given to the town in 1861 by Phoebe Locke in memory of her husband Joseph Locke, a renowned mathematician, engineer and railway builder educated at Barnsley Grammar School. The park affords a fine prospect of Barnsley, the centre of the Yorkshire coalfield. As well as being known for coal mining, Barnsley was the country's greatest linen producer during the nineteenth century and a major manufacturer of glass.

Left The Mansion House at Doncaster is one of only three such buildings in England, the others being in York and London. It was designed in the 1740s by James Paine for the mayor, to use both as a residence and for official functions. Although no mayor has lived there since 1840, the building still retains its grandeur in the shape of the Grand Staircase, the Ballroom and William Lindley's Banqueting Hall, added in 1806 and used as the venue for the Dinner which follows the St Leger, a race first run in 1776. Rich in charters, the first being granted by Richard I in 1194, Doncaster can boast a full list of mayors from 1493. The town was founded as a Roman fort on the line of Watling Street and by the end of the eighteenth century the Mansion House would have been a familiar sight to travellers on the Great North Road, for which Doncaster was a coaching stop. A century later it was a canal and rail centre and home to the Great Northern Railway Workshops. It remains to this day a busy centre at the heart of South Yorkshire's communication network.

Right The Church of St George at Doncaster, built in 1854-8 and considered by historian Sir Nikolaus Pevsner to be 'the proudest and most cathedral-like' of all Sir George Gilbert Scott's parish churches. It replaced a medieval predecessor which burned down in 1853, despite a plea for assistance being sent by train to Swinton near Rotherham, from where word was telegraphed to Sheffield. Under the vestry, far below the 170 feet high central tower, the vaulted crypt of the original church survives.

The Dutch River, looking east from Rawcliffe Bridge across flatlands to the cranes of Goole Docks. It was constructed in 1633 by Dutchman Cornelius Vermuyden as part of Charles I's ambitious drainage scheme to create 60,000 acres of arable land from what, at the time, was a vast wetland wilderness encompassing the royal hunting estate of Hatfield Chase. Previously the Don had emptied into the Trent and Aire, causing extensive flooding, and the new river carried the Don from near Snaith in a six mile straight line directly into the Ouse at Goole. Despite subsequent peat extraction on a huge scale, nearby Thorne Moors survives as the best example of a raised sphagnum bog left in Britain, providing a habitat for rare insects, plants, and birds such as the elusive nightjar.

THE VALE OF YORK

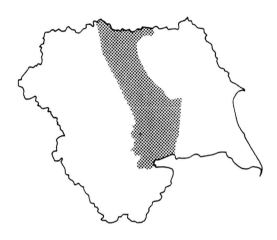

THE Vale of York stretches like a slender sixty mile long corridor from the borders of South Yorkshire northwards to the River Tees. Once an area of impassable marshland that could only be safely crossed by way of a raised ridge to the south of York, its glacial boulder clay and alluvial soils today provide good rich farmland which extends from the foothills of the Dales to the slopes of the North York Moors and Wolds. The centre of the Vale is cut by the Great North Road (now the A1), whilst into it run the five great northern Yorkshire rivers: the Swale, Ure, Nidd, Wharfe and Derwent – all of which meander lazily across the countryside to eventually form the Ouse and flow east into the North Sea. Many of England's greatest battles – Marston Moor, Stamford Bridge, the Battle of the Standard and Towton – were fought here, another indication of the strategic importance of this ancient thoroughfare.

The Swale spends nearly half of its seventy mile course in the Vale after leaving the narrow confines of its dale at Richmond. The river and the modern A1 run virtually side-by-side down to the vicinity of the former coaching towns of Northallerton, Thirsk and Boroughbridge. At its narrowest point, in the so-called Vale of Mowbray around Northallerton, the Vale receives the waters of the Wiske and the Cod Beck from the Cleveland and Hambleton Hills before they too unite and enter the Swale near Topcliffe. Near the Roman town of Boroughbridge, at the attractive village of Myton-on-Swale – typical of many in the Vale, with its red-tiled cottages and orchards – the Swale merges with the Ure, and a tiny insignificant stream, rising at Ouseburn, which gives its name to the now broad and silty river which passes through York. Between here and the foot of the Howardian Hills, was once the Forest of Galtres, through whose branches at dusk travellers looked nervously for lanterns hung in the towers of York's churches to guide them safely away from the wolves and brigands that lived in the Forest.

Around York the Vale broadens to about thirty miles. The city was founded where a Roman road crossed the Ouse, and it's influence over much of northern England is underlined by the remains of Roman 'Eboracum' as well as Viking 'Jorvik'. Today it is arguably Europe's finest walled city; a treasure house which encapsulates much of England's history. Within its walls are a maze of old-world streets, elegant Georgian buildings, a ruined Norman abbey, and the largest medieval cathedral in Europe.

Between York and the port of Goole at the head of the Humber Estuary the Ouse runs a deep, sluggish, and muddy course. The Wharfe enters it at Cawood, and between Selby and Goole it is swollen by another tributary, the Derwent. Although the landscape at this southern end of the Vale is less spectacular, it is steeped in history. Selby Abbey, Birkin and Stillingfleet churches are all Norman. The Archbishops of York had palaces at Bishopthorpe and Cawood. Close to Goole the Ouse absorbs the murky waters of the Aire, both rivers being tidal far back into the county.

Previous page The magnificent Rose Window in the South Transept of York Minster, dating from the early sixteenth century and thought to commemorate the marriage of Henry VII and Elizabeth of York in 1486 which united the Houses of York and Lancaster – hence the white and red roses in the window's outer 'petals'.

Kiplin Hall on the Swale near Catterick, built in about 1620 by Sir George Calvert, Secretary of State to James I. The Jacobean Hall is built in mellow brick and is said to be based on early designs by Inigo Jones while working in Denmark. In 1632 Calvert was granted land by Charles I to found the Catholic colony of Maryland in America, named in honour of the Queen, Henrietta Maria. Although he died soon after, one of his sons fulfilled his plan by leaving Yorkshire with 300 colonists, many from the nearby 'archer's village' of Scorton.

The sixteenth century pink sandstone tower of St Mary's Church in the quiet village of Bolton-on-Swale near Catterick. The pyramid-shaped headstone on the left commemorates the legendary Henry Jenkins, claimed to have died here in 1670 at the age of 169. Jenkins was born in 1500 and his earliest memory was of carrying arrows for the English bowmen at Flodden Field in 1513. He was a fisherman for 140 years, swam the local rivers in his hundreds, was still harvesting at 160 and lived through the reigns of ten monarchs.

Left The broad half-mile long High Street in Northallerton, a busy and prosperous market town, and administrative centre of the North Riding. There was a Roman settlement here and nearby on the Darlington Road is an obelisk which marks the site of the Battle of the Standard, where in 1138 the invading Scots were decimated by a hail of English arrows. Although now happily bypassed, the town became a popular halt on the coaching route between Boroughbridge and Durham, and is consequently well supplied with hotels and inns, notably the Old Fleece – which charmed Dickens – and the Golden Lion.

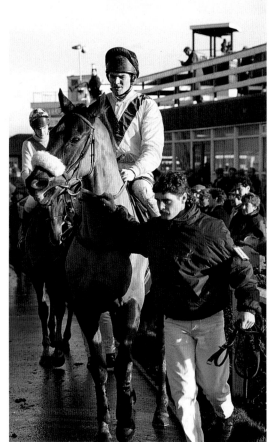

Left Jockeys and their horses in the paddock at Catterick Racecourse, which was opened in 1783. As well as being a nationally famous racing venue, Catterick is also known for its RAF and army garrison, a tradition stretching back to Roman times when it was the military station of *Cataractonium*. The Emperor Paulinus came here in the seventh century to baptise thousands of Christian converts in the nearby Swale. Catterick straddles the Great North Road and was once a major coaching stop. The Victorian landlord of one of its many inns, the Bridge House Hotel, once cleared the snow-covered racecourse by driving his sheep round it!

Right The pilot of a Tornado F3 of XI Squadron climbs aboard after ground crew have prepared the aircraft for take-off at Royal Air Force Leeming. XI Squadron was formed during the Great War and had a distinguished record in both World Wars. It became based at Leeming in 1988 and flew vital combat air patrols on the Saudi-Iraq border during the Gulf War. Leeming itself opened in 1940 as a base for Bomber Command and took on its present major NATO Air Defence Fighter role in 1982. Its aircraft have long been on the front line, flying Combat Air Patrols over the North Sea in search of Soviet reconnaissance aircraft, many of which they have successfully escorted out of British airspace.

Below The charming village of Crayke, perched on the edge of the Howardian Hills overlooking the Vale of York. Beyond the village well and cottages is the medieval Church of St Cuthbert, occupying a site where the saint's body is said to have rested in the ninth century while on its journey from Lindisfarne to its eventual resting place in Durham Cathedral. Out of view, behind the church, is Crayke Castle, a thirteenth century tower house built on the site of a Norman motte-and-bailey. It once belonged to the Prince Bishops of Durham (hence the village's 'Durham Ox' inn) and remained a part of County Durham until incorporated into Yorkshire by Act of Parliament in 1844.

Right The Market Place, Thirsk, through which passes Cod Beck, a tributary of the Swale running in the lee of the Hambleton Hills. The surrounding fertile countryside is the setting for the novels by the late James Herriot, based on his real-life experiences as a vet in the town.

Below right Two of the three surviving standing stones, known as the Devil's Arrows, which stand in a cornfield between the A1 and the old coaching town of Boroughbridge. Between 18 and 22 feet high and weighing nearly 40 tons apiece, the stones were dragged here six miles from gritstone quarries at Knaresborough. They are aligned north-south and are thought to have been part of a Neolithic/Early Bronze Age ceremonial site contemporary with Stonehenge. Early antiquarians mention other stones and there are associated earthworks stretching to Ripon and beyond. Until the eighteenth century the Fair of St Barnabas was held here on Midsummer's Day, a reminder of some ancient ritual. The stones owe their name to a legend in which they were thrown by the Devil from Howe Hill only to fall short of his intended target, the Christian settlement at Aldborough.

York Minster towering above the City's rooftops as seen from the medieval walls. One tower sports some of the seemingly permanent shroud of scaffolding as the historic fabric is cleaned and restored. The Minster occupies not only the site of the Roman military headquarters of the 'colonia' of Eboracum, founded in AD 71, but also of a wooden temple, built as early as 627, where the Saxon King Edwin of Northumbria was baptised by Paulinus, first Archbishop of York. The Normans under Archbishop Thomas of Bayeux began building the Minster late in the eleventh century, although it did not reach its present form until 1480, by which time the Norman structure had been all but replaced. The oldest sections visible above ground are the Early English transepts, dating from the mid-thirteenth century, and the vast Decorated nave begun in 1291. The choir was built around 1400, the great Perpendicular central tower in the early fifteenth century, and the western towers in about 1450. The building, which is the largest Gothic cathedral in Europe, thus embraces the entire evolution of English ecclesiastical Gothic architecture.

The Great East Window above the Lady Chapel in York Minster, created between 1405-1408 by master glass painter John Thornton of Coventry. On the right is St. William's College built between 1455-67 by George Neville, later Archbishop, and his brother the Earl of Warwick, to house the Minster's twenty three chantry priests. A doorway leads through to a delightful quadrangle of stone buildings with timbered upper floors jettied out on carved brackets. In the background is the Minster's octagonal Chapter House built between 1286-1307 and containing a Latin inscription which describes the Minster as 'the house of houses, as the rose is the flower of flowers'.

A striking view of Clifford's Tower on the north bank of the Ouse at York, originally built as a castle on the site of a wooden palisade erected by William the Conqueror in 1068, together with another on the south bank. It was burned by the Danes in 1089 and again during riots in 1190 when Jews taking refuge in it were massacred. It was rebuilt in stone by Henry III after his visit in 1244 as part of the medieval city defences, which enclosed an area five times that of the Roman fortress and of which 4 main gates, 39 towers and 3 miles of wall survive. The tower is today named after Henry Clifford, 5th Earl of Cumberland and hereditary constable of the castle, who rebuilt it in 1642 in readiness for a Parliamentarian siege of the Royalist city in 1644. Afterwards it continued as a prison and court, and today overlooks the Castle Museum.

The ruins of St. Mary's Abbey which, together with the medieval St. Leonard's Hospital and the medieval Multangular Tower atop a portion of original Roman walling, are to be found in the lovely gardens of the Yorkshire Museum at York. Once the foremost Benedictine house in the north of England, St. Mary's was founded in 1089 by William Rufus just outside the city walls on the north bank of the Ouse. In 1132 after an argument with the Archbishop over lax discipline the then prior left to found Fountains Abbey. By the late thirteenth century the original Norman church had been wholly rebuilt then surrounded by a towered precinct wall, only to be breached during the Civil War in 1644. Today only a few walls remain but every few years they provide the perfect backdrop for a performance of the famous York Mystery plays, a biblical history of the world once enacted by the local guildsmen on the backs of waggons.

Left Members of the York City Rowing Club approaching Lendal Bridge past the City Guildhall (centre) on the banks of the Ouse. The Guildhall was built by the Corporation in 1449-54 and is one of four such surviving medieval halls in York. They were used as administrative centres for the various guilds of merchants and craftsmen involved in the export of local products along the Ouse during the later middle ages. Such trade brought great prosperity and made York England's second city, although its monopoly as an inland port was short-lived as other rivers were made navigable. On the left, with a corner turret, are the Victorian Municipal Offices mimicking the style of the much older Guildhall.

Below Looking up Stonegate towards York Minster along which the stone used in the Minsters construction may have been carried. Some six feet below the present surface lies the *Via Praetoria* which led from a gateway in St. Helen's Square to the Roman military headquarters, where today sits the Minster. It was the Danes who laid out many of York's streets, known as 'gates', as well as the gateways they called 'bars'. Most of the city's building periods from the fifteenth century are still represented here, including some fine shop frontages. The Olde Starre Inn built in 1644 remains York's oldest public house.

Below Neat and tidy gift shops today occupy The Shambles in York, a far cry from the dirty and noisy medieval 'street of the butchers' where animals were slaughtered on the spot and hung out for sale. The Shambles is but one of a warren of narrow streets known locally as 'snickelways', which occupied this part of the medieval Tudor town. At one point the overhanging timbered upper storeys are so close that the occupier could shake hands with their neighbour.

The Mansion House overlooking St. Helen's Square in York was begun in 1726 and, like those of Doncaster and London, was built as the official residence of the Lord Mayor during his term of office and to provide a venue for civic functions. The first incumbent was John Stainforth in 1730 and its architect, said to be Lord Burlington, was made an honorary freeman in gratitude for providing York with one of its most attractive buildings. Together with other well-proportioned eighteenth century public buildings, the Mansion House reflects a period of artistic appreciation and gracious living when the city exceeded Bath as a centre of fashion. On the right is the Yorkshire Insurance building of 1840 as well as the brick-built post office.

Sir Nigel Gresley's celebrated locomotive 'Mallard', which achieved the world speed record of 126 miles per hour for a steam engine in 1938, surrounded by a handful of the ninety or so engines and carriages in the National Railway Museum, York. The collection was established in 1975 in a former rail depot, nearly fifty years after Britain's first railway museum had been founded here. The city was an obvious choice, having been an important nineteenth century railway centre where George Hudson (1800-1871), the 'Railway King', had built up his great Victorian rail empire stretching to Newcastle and Edinburgh. As well as engines there is much rolling stock including several luxuriously appointed royal coaches.

Above When the famous Yorkshire thatcher Seth Eccles retired, Wiltshireman William Tegetmeier decided to carry on the ancient tradition. Now a Master Thatcher, he and his young Journeyman Aron Greenwood (seen here) are the only thatchers working in North East England. Their business takes them from East Anglia up to the Scottish Borders, whilst virtually every thatched cottage in Yorkshire has benefited from their skill. After working on this cottage throughout the winter they are now putting the finishing touches to the reed thatch by adding a straw roof ridge.

Above The narrowboat *Serendipity* passing through Naburn Lock on its way down the Ouse just south of York. During the early eighteenth century many of Yorkshire's rivers, such as the Aire, Calder and Derwent, were made navigable, eroding York's historical supremacy as a port. This was halted, albeit temporarily, by the construction in 1757 of Naburn Lock, raising the draught at York by a metre and a half. Just visible in the trees on the right is the Banqueting House, built in 1823 as a meeting place for the Ouse Navigation Trustees.

Below John Smith's massive Magnet Brewery, dominating the skyline of the market town of Tadcaster. The convenient local supply of high quality hard water enabled a brewery to be established here in 1758. It was bought by John Smith in 1847 and passed to his brother Samuel whose Old Brewery still exists on the High Street. Another brother, William, built the present Magnet Brewery in 1883, taking with him the John Smith name. The brewery is now owned by Courage Breweries, and produces, on average, 1 ½ million barrels of beer a year.

Right The superb south doorway of the Church of St Helen at Stillingfleet near York, one of several fine Norman churches in the area. As well as the elaborate stonework, the wooden door itself is of interest with its great C-shaped iron hinges. Towards the top, and also in iron strapwork, can be seen a Viking-style boat and two figures. Some say they allude to the Danish flotilla of Tostig and Harold Hardrada which sailed up the Humber in 1066 prior to its defeat at the Battle of Stamford Bridge. It is also said that traces of human skin were once found beneath the ironwork.

Below Cawood Castle on the Ouse near Selby, built in limestone quarried from near Tadcaster, for which Cawood acted as a distribution point. The Castle was a victim of the Civil War, and only the fifteenth century gatehouse remains of what was once a palace of the Archbishops of York. Medieval archbishops lived in a style to match their status. When George Neville became Archbishop in 1456 he gave a banquet at Cawood at which the guests consumed 100 oxen and curlews, 200 pheasants, 400 swans, woodcocks and plovers, 500 deer and partridges, 600 pike and bream, 1,000 sheep and capons, 2,000 pigs, geese and chickens, 4,000 rabbits, ducks and pigeons, and 5,000 venison pasties and custards– all washed down with 400 barrels of ale and wine. It was also at Cawood that in 1530 Cardinal Wolsey, then Lord Chancellor, was arrested on a charge of high treason for failing to support Henry VIII in his wish to exchange Catherine of Aragon for Anne Boleyn as his queen.

Left The elegant 13th century 190 feet spire of the Church of St Mary at Hemingbrough, near Selby. Originally a simple, aisle-less Anglo-Saxon church, like nearby Howden it had associations with the Prince Bishops of Durham. The chancel and fine East Window, as well as Sir John West's ornate chantry chapel, add lustre to a building whose glorious medieval woodwork includes a misericord thought to be the oldest in England.

Below left Late afternoon sunlight illuminating the limestone west front of Selby Abbey. Dominating the market place, its origins lie in a monastery church built to serve a Benedictine community established here in the late eleventh century. Benedict of Auxerre chose Selby after interpreting the sight of three swans on the River Ouse as the fulfilment of an earlier vision. The west doorway is one of several Norman elements later incorporated into the predominantly Gothic building. Fortunately it survived the Dissolution to serve as the parish church for what became a shipbuilding port with its own canal connecting the Ouse and the Aire. Although the great central tower fell in 1690 and fire swept the Abbey in 1906, by 1935 it had been restored to its former glory.

Opposite page top Stamford Bridge, at the junction of the River Derwent with the York-Bridlington road, and close to the site of the last Saxon victory in England. It was here, in September 1066, that the doomed King Harold came face to face with his brother Tostig and Harold Hardrada, the King of Norway. Harold offered Tostig a third of England in return for peace; but would only give Harold Hardrada seven feet of soil, and that for his grave! The offer was refused and both Earl Tostig and Harold Hardrada were killed in the ensuing battle. It is said the Derwent ran red with blood, and of the 500 ships which brought the invading army only 20 returned home with the survivors. For Harold victory was brief, for he met his death soon after at Hastings against William of Normandy and his conquering army.

Opposite page bottom Old lock buildings and the fourteenth century tower of St Michael's Church at Sutton upon Derwent, below Elvington Bridge on the River Derwent. From 1701 onwards much of the 75 mile river was gradually made navigable to transport agricultural produce, timber, coal and lime as far as Malton. Above this point the river ceases to be tidal, hence the construction of the lock. The present mechanism was installed in 1938 and is one of the few guillotine gates in Yorkshire.

Left Children examining Britain's largest sundial on a cottage in Seaton Ross, a village near Holme upon Spalding Moor. Boasting a diameter of 12 feet, it was the work of local farmer and sundial enthusiast William Watson (1784-1857). He placed another sundial on the wall of his own farm and a third in St Edmund's Church – where his own tombstone is inscribed: 'At this church I so often with pleasure did call, That I made a sundial upon the church wall'.

Below Geoff Morton of Hasholme Carr Farm at Holme upon Spalding Moor is these days a rare breed of farmer. He maintains thirty working horses (Shires, Clydesdales, Percherons and Ardennes) on his small farm on the edge of the Vale of York, using them in ways that would have been commonplace throughout much of rural Yorkshire until mechanisation took over after the last war.

Opposite page The peaceful 9½ mile long Pocklington Canal at Hagg Bridge, meandering through rich countryside just prior to joining the River Derwent via the East Cottingwith entrance lock. Opened in 1818 to carry agricultural produce to the industrial towns of South and West Yorkshire, it was also used to bring lime and coal to Pocklington. Unusually for a canal it cost less to construct than anticipated. It was sold in 1847 to the York and North Midland Railway and was last used commercially in 1932. Despite a period of decline its locks and swing-bridges have now been restored.

Wressle Castle, on the River Derwent between
Selby and Howden. The only fortified dwelling in
the old East Riding, it was built in 1380 for Sir
Thomas Percy, Earl of Worcester, using, it is said,
stone brought from France. Only the shell of the
south range now remains, set between two towers
housing the hall and chapel. The historian Leland
described it as being 'all of very fair and great
squared stone'. In 1403 Percy was taken prisoner at
the Battle of Shrewsbury and beheaded, after which
the Castle passed to the powerful Northumberland
the family. During the Civil War it was garrisoned
with Parliamentarian troops and later partially
demolished.

THE WOLDS AND
HOLDERNESS

THE WOLDS AND HOLDERNESS

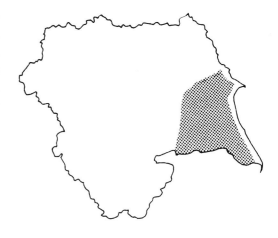

DESCRIBED by Daniel Defoe in the early eighteenth century as 'thin of towns, and consequently of people', East Yorkshire's Wolds remain an area of gentle, rolling uplands. Geologically they are composed of the youngest rocks in Yorkshire, the chalk laid down in the shallow sea that covered most of the county some 150 million years ago. The chalk forms a crescent of high land between Flamborough in the east – where it ends spectacularly in sheer cliffs – and Hessle on the Humber Estuary in the south-west. Compared to Yorkshire's other hills these are small, reaching only 654 feet at Settrington Beacon. They are everywhere cut by characteristic dry valleys, the surface water which formed them having subsequently seeped through the porous chalk. Where streams do exist they are intermittent and temporary affairs known as 'Gypseys', and only run in the wake of heavy rain. The best known is the Gypsey Race, which flows from near Rudston to Bridlington Harbour, and whose appearance has traditionally been regarded as an omen of imminent disaster. The lack of surface water in the Wolds has always been a concern, and one solved by many villages having ponds, which in turn add to the distinctive character of the region.

During the Middle Ages much of the area was transformed into one vast sheep run and the once rich arable land became pasture for grazing. The impact was catastrophic. Combined with the effects of the Black Death, the area became so depopulated that one in six of the villages named in the Domesday Book was abandoned or deserted. During

Previous page The village of Warter set in a typical Wolds landscape.

Left Some 80 or so varieties of water lily are to be found at Burnby Hall Gardens near Pocklington, on the western edge of the Wolds, making it the most outstanding collection of its kind in Europe. The house and gardens were bequeathed to the town on the death of its owner, Major Percy Marlborough Stewart (1871-1962), a godson of the Duke of Marlborough and an adventurer who, together with his wife, travelled the world before settling here. A museum houses the trophies and souvenirs from his global wanderings. The lakes were originally formed to indulge a passion for fishing, but after his wife suggested that a few water plants might be an attractive addition he embarked on the creation of these remarkable and unique water gardens.

the eighteenth century great landowners such as Sir Christopher Sykes of Sledmere 'made the Wolds' barren waste fertile' by extensive ploughing and road building, once again transforming a backward area into fine arable land. The early stages of the Enclosure of England's agricultural land occurred here, culminating in today's seemingly endless fields of barley and wheat. There are few towns of any size on the Wolds apart from Great Driffield, its 'capital', with a weekly cattle market and former canal which once took grain to Hull, and the rest of the region consists of a scatter of quiet unspoilt villages such as Boynton, Harpham, North Dalton and Fimber. The two other large towns of Pocklington and Market Weighton – whose canal once carried locally made bricks to Hull – are situated at the foot of the Wolds where the land falls away to the River Derwent and Vale of York. This gentle land is a bird watchers' paradise of water meadows, reedy dykes and disused canals. The Minster of Howden rises out of this fertile fenland, its bold square tower contrasting with the narrow spire of Goole church across the wide bend of the Ouse.

Contained within the arc of the chalk hills to the south and the east where it is bounded by the North Sea and the Humber lies the area described by Chaucer in *The Canterbury Tales* as the 'mersshy country called Holdernesse'. A thick layer of glacial boulder clay which has been drained and reclaimed over the centuries, it is now fertile farmland where oats and barley thrive. Fine country houses such as Burton Constable, together with the now-oversized churches at the silted-up former ports of Hedon and Patrington, bear witness to the prosperity of its original farmers and merchants. The once important port of Beverley, with its Gothic Minster, dominates the landscape in the heart of the area. Hull, which used to boast one of the world's largest fishing fleets, is today an important European ferry and container-ship terminal. Similarly Goole, still an important port, which used to export Yorkshire coal, has had to diversify and adapt by handling other cargoes. The Humber Estuary itself – which drains around one fifth of England – is today crossed by the graceful single-span Humber Bridge; a far cry indeed from the humble ferry used by the Romans to connect Lincoln with East Yorkshire.

Thatched cottages border the village green at Warter, a pretty Victorian estate village on the south-western edge of the Wolds. An Augustinian Priory originally existed here, and its foundations are still visible near the church. After the Dissolution, the Pennington family from Muncaster Castle in Cumberland built a hall here and gradually converted the neighbouring settlement into an estate village, reducing its size to lessen repair costs. In 1878 the Hull shipping magnate Charles Wilson purchased the estate and transformed its shabby mud and timber houses into a neat group of brick and slate buildings with ornate woodwork. Although the hall, once boasting a hundred rooms, has been demolished, Warter retains an air of quiet elegance to this day.

The ruined church of St Martin beside the old millpond in the deserted medieval village of Wharram Percy near Sledmere. One in six Wolds villages are now deserted, due mainly to the switch from labour intensive crop growing to the grazing of sheep for wool production in the Tudor period. Wharram Percy, named after the fourteenth century lords of the manor, is unusual in that it has been thoroughly excavated by the Medieval Village Research Group, providing a valuable portrait of settlement and rural life from the Neolithic period up to the sixteenth century. The church, founded in the Anglo-Saxon period, continued to be in regular use until the 1940s and today one special service is held each year in the ruins.

Left The prehistoric mound of Duggleby Howe, near Sledmere in the northern Wolds. One of the largest in Britain, the 20 feet high barrow contains 5,000 tons of chalk and measures 120 feet across. It was found to contain some 50 cremation burials accompanied by bone pins and flint implements of the Late Neolithic period (2,500-2,000 BC). The gentle, well-drained chalk of the Wolds is one of the richest areas in Yorkshire for such vestiges of early man's activities.

Below left The Staircase Hall at Sledmere House, on the northern Wolds near Driffield. Originally a medieval manor house, the present building was begun by Richard Sykes (1678-1726) when he married Mary Kirkby, the heiress of Sledmere. In 1776 it was inherited by his nephew Sir Christopher Sykes (1749-1801), the agricultural reformer, who extended the house, added the 100 feet long library, and employed 'Capability' Brown to landscape the surrounding park. Much of the decorated plasterwork is by the Yorkshire plasterer Joseph Rose who had worked with the famous Robert Adam. The running frieze in the Staircase Hall shows the alternating arms of the Kirkby and Sykes families. More recent members of the family include Lieutenant Colonel Mark Sykes (1879-1919), responsible for raising the Wolds Wagoners – a special transport corps of local farm workers – for the Expeditionary Force to France in the Great War. Although the house was gutted by fire in 1911 it was carefully restored for the family by Walter Brierley as an elegant Georgian country house but with a contemporary Edwardian grandeur.

Opposite page An old steam-powered corn mill and a pair of Victorian cranes mark the head of the Driffield Navigation. The market town of Great Driffield has for centuries lain at the heart of an important agricultural area, giving rise to the name 'Capital of the Wolds'. Exports to Hull were once only possible down the awkward River Hull until the canal was opened in 1770. Although now disused, the canal brought considerable prosperity to a town noted for its markets, horse sales, mills (several of which still operate) and breweries.

A classic Yorkshire Wolds landscape of open fields and rolling chalk hills divided by dry valleys, looking south-east along the valley of Crake Dale towards Langtoft in the northern Wolds. Until the nineteenth century much of the Wolds was one vast sheep run, but more recently the original fields have been replanted with more profitable arable crops such as barley.

The Norman Church of St Andrew at Weaverthorpe in the northern Wolds, its tall tower reached by an external staircase turret. A Saxon sundial over the south doorway bears an inscription which tells us that the church was built by Herbert the Chamberlain, of Winchester. It was restored for Sir Tatton Sykes of Sledmere in 1872 by George Edmund Street who designed the brightly painted barrel roof which adorns the otherwise austere interior. Despite its restoration the little church at Weaverthorpe remains virtually the same as it would have appeared to the Wolds country folk of the twelfth century.

Below A small part of the glorious painted interior of St Michael's Church at Garton-on-the-Wolds, near Driffield. The church was established by Kirkham Priory in about 1130 and several Norman features remain. It was restored for local landowner Sir Tatton Sykes (the fourth of that name) of Sledmere by Gothic Revivalist John Loughborough Pearson in 1856, whilst a second restoration by Edmund Street in 1865 under the patronage of the fifth Sir Tatton included the lavish and quite stunning thirteenth century style wall paintings. Executed by Clayton and Bell, who had worked at Westminster Abbey, they cover every inch of available wall space in an unparalleled variety of Old and New Testament scenes. The wall between nave and chancel (pictured here) depicts the Virgin and Child at the top of the Tree of Jesse, the symbolic representation of the ancestry of Christ from Jesse the father of King David, as set out in St Matthew's Gospel. The paintings themselves were restored between 1986 and 1991 in memory of the architectural historian Sir Nikolaus Pevsner and now look as fresh as the day they were painted.

Above The South Front of Burton Agnes Hall near Driffield, built for Sir Henry Griffith, a member of the Council of the North, between 1601 and 1610. The architect was Robert Smythson, who had worked at Longleat and Hardwick Hall. The red brick Elizabethan mansion, with its stone detailing, bay windows and typically tall, clustered chimneys, passed in 1654 to the Boynton family, who have lived here ever since. It contains a fine collection of French Impressionist paintings and Chippendale furniture, as well as many of its original decorated ceilings and carved fireplaces.

Right All Saints churchyard at Rudston, near Bridlington, dominated by its prehistoric monolith which, at over 25 feet high, is Britain's tallest standing stone. It is made of a grey gritstone which originated at Cayton Bay some 10 miles to the north, and is believed to have been erected as part of an ancient ceremonial site (ditches and tumuli abound in the surrounding countryside). The Norman church is in fact youthful compared to the monolith, which has been dated to the late Neolithic/Early Bronze Age period, making it some 4,000 years old. Also in the churchyard is the grave of Rudston born Winifred Holtby, author of *South Riding* and *The Land of Green Ginger*, who died in 1935 at the age of 37.

"Happy, oh happy, oh happy are we
Living in Walkington, you and me.
Of this pretty village we're all very fond
Three pubs and a church and a mucky 'owd pond"

So runs 'The Walkington Song', one of many which accompany the Victorian Hayride at Walkington near Beverley. The Hayride has taken place every June since 1967 as a way of raising money for charity by displaying the style and transport of Victorian country people. The leading wagon in the procession is a genuine vintage Wolds Wagon loaned by heavy horse farmer Geoff Morton from nearby Holme upon Spalding Moor. It carries the colourful and exuberant founder of the Hayride, Ernie Teal (known by all as 'Mr Walkington'), here resplendent in red military jacket, as the cavalcade passes the 'mucky owd pond' on its way to Bishop Burton and Beverley.

The sails of Yorkshire's last fully working tower windmill at Skidby receiving a new coat of paint. It was built in 1821 by Gartons of Beverley for William Watson and was once one of many in the breezy arable Wolds of East Yorkshire. Between 1854 and the 1960s it was run by Joseph Thompson and family who retained its workings intact despite the introduction of electricity in 1947. Beverley Borough Council have subsequently renovated the mill as a working museum and it continues to attract thousands of visitors each year.

Above The magnificent west front of Beverley
Minster as seen from the Westwood, one of four
Common Pastures which provide a green belt
around this most attractive of market towns.
According to the Venerable Bede, a monastery was
founded here in the seventh century by St John of
Beverley, although the present Minster dates from
the thirteenth and fifteenth centuries. The twin
towers represent the finest example of Gothic
Perpendicular work, their bells sounding the
quarters in the north tower and the hours in the
south. Other superlatives include the fine set of
misericord seats, the splendid Gothic Decorated
funerary monument in the shape of the Percy
Tomb, and a unique series of minstrel carvings. An
unusual feature is the Anglo-Saxon 'frith stool'
which provided the right of sanctuary as endowed
by King Athelstan in thanks for his victory against
the Scots and Danes at the Battle of Brunanburh in
937.

Right A medieval citole player looking down into
the north aisle of Beverley Minster, just one of the
seventy stone carvings of medieval instruments on
the aisle arches in the Minster, and which together
form the largest such collection in the world. Along
with a series of similar carvings in St Mary's
Church they date back to the time when Beverley
was the headquarters of the Minstrels' Guild of
Northern England who met annually in the town to
choose an alderman.

Below The busy Saturday Market around the Market Cross at Beverley, East Yorkshire's oldest town. Meaning 'beavers' stream', Beverley grew from an Anglo-Saxon monastery founded by St John of Beverley, Archbishop of York. Although sacked by the Danes it was refounded in 932 along with a Minster Church to serve the growing community. Throughout the Middle Ages it prospered from the wool trade and as a place of pilgrimage, becoming one of England's wealthiest towns. In Georgian and Victorian times its industries included tanning, founding and engineering, and many fine terraces were built. Towering over the square is St Mary's Church, which contains the carving of a rabbit believed to have inspired Lewis Carroll to create the March Hare in *Alice in Wonderland*.

Right St Peter's Church at Howden, seen from one of the quiet market town's cobbled streets. In medieval times Howden was the centre of a great parish known as 'Howdenshire', controlled by the Prince Bishops of Durham who had a palace here. During the fourteenth and fifteenth centuries the church was rebuilt in fine Tadcaster limestone and given its tower – more glass than wall – by Bishop Skirlaw of Durham. After the Dissolution in 1538 the townspeople took over the church but could not afford the upkeep. Consequently the chancel and chapter house collapsed leaving the tower rising from the ruins.

Opposite page top The Humber Bridge, the world's largest single-span suspension bridge, looking southwards from Hessle across the deep Humber Estuary, to Barton-upon-Humber. The 2,428 yard long bridge was opened by the Queen in July 1981, 22 years after the Humber Bridge Act had been passed. Prior to building the bridge, the only way across the river had been the hourly paddle-steamer to Hull or else the 35 mile drive around the estuary. The Humber, one of Britain's great commercial waterways since the Middle Ages, still represents a spiritual boundary between Yorkshire and Lincolnshire, as witnessed by the failure of the new county of Humberside.

Opposite page bottom The busy sea port of Goole, purpose-built in 1826 by the Aire and Calder Navigation Company at the end of their canal extension from Knottingley. Goole, previously a small village, gradually flourished as a centre for the import of raw materials, but more importantly for the export of goods from the industrial areas of Yorkshire, notably coal to London. The hydraulic hoist on the right was designed specifically to lift coal barges, known as 'Tom Puddings', from the canal and to empty their contents into awaiting colliers. Goole continues to be an important port handling mixed cargoes to and from the Continent.

Left A freighter being unloaded of its cargo, with dawn breaking over the Albert Dock in Hull. Yorkshire's major seaport was originally founded by Cistercian monks from Meaux Abbey as the town of Wyke-upon-Humber, at the point where the River Hull joins the Humber, growing rich on its trade in wool, leather and wine. Edward I recognized its potential and acquired the town in 1293, changing its name to Kingestown-upon-Hull and making it a free borough by Royal Charter. The Civil War brought the city prominence when it refused entry to Charles I, but friendly relations with Charles II heralded new prosperity. In 1773 the Dock Company was founded and the medieval defensive moats surrounding the Old Town were replaced by a series of docks. Hull expanded rapidly, becoming the centre of the whaling industry and home port to the world's largest fishing fleet. Today it handles a wide array of container freight, bulk cargo and ferry traffic, trading on its position at the junction of the Ouse, the Trent and the North Sea.

Far left The Trinity House of Hull, which began life as a religious fraternity called the Guild of the Holy Trinity. One of five Trinity House Corporations given charters by Henry VIII after the Dissolution it became a seamans' guild in 1456. During the seventeenth and eighteenth centuries it controlled shipping and navigation in the Humber area. The present building was erected in 1753 and contains a fine former courtroom, adorned with model ships, and a navigation school. The pediment over the door depicts Neptune and Britannia flanking the Royal coat of arms.

Left The Great Nave of Holy Trinity Church in the old Market Place at Hull, said, in terms of floor area, to be England's largest parish church. Built to serve an increasingly prosperous merchant community, the transepts and chancel belong to the early fourteenth century. After a delay due to the Black Death work on the nave continued into the early fifteenth century. The 150 feet central tower is supported by four great oak rafts constructed to prevent the tower sinking into the underlying clay. The brickwork in the transepts represents the first major use of brick in medieval England.

Above The lighthouse at Paull, a former fishing village overlooking the Humber Estuary. Prior to its construction in 1836 by the seamans' guild of Trinity House in Hull, a lantern was lit nightly in a rented room above the Humber Tavern to guide shipping up the estuary.

Right The so-called Ravenspurn Cross, in the grounds of Holyrood House, Hedon. The seaport of Ravenspurn once lay to the east of Spurn Point and is said to have been where the Danes planted their standard, 'the Raven', following their landing in 867. Briefly a wealthy port electing two members of Parliament, it was washed away at the end of the fifteenth century and all that remains is the Cross and its church bells, which now hang at Easington and Aldborough.

The east front of Burton Constable Hall in Holderness, a Tudor mansion built originally between 1570 and 1600, and remodelled in the Georgian period by the then owner, William Constable. The embattled corner towers of the original hall can still be made out at each end, whilst the lack of a native stone in Holderness meant that the whole building was built in brick.

A classic English scene, as cricket is played beneath the 189 feet high spire of St Patrick's Church in the village of Patrington. Known as the 'Queen of Holderness' (St Augustine's at Hedon being 'the King') this fourteenth century building is one of the most magnificent parish churches in England, providing a striking landmark in the surrounding flat countryside. One of the first accounts of cricket in Yorkshire refers to a game played at Sheffield in 1751 for which the authorities hired professional players to amuse the locals and so entice them away from cock-fighting!

THE NORTH YORK MOORS AND THE VALE OF PICKERING

THE NORTH YORK MOORS AND THE VALE OF PICKERING

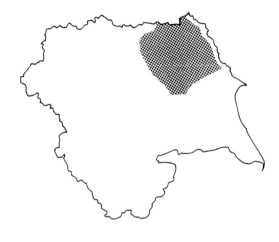

IN the seventh century England's first historian, the Venerable Bede, described the North York Moors as 'steep and solitary hills where you would rather look for the hiding places of robbers or lairs of wild animals than the abode of men.' Although the area has been a National Park since 1952, it still retains a wild aspect, being both dramatic and sparsely populated. Much is a high plateau of sandstone moorland bounded by escarpments in the north, west, and south, and ending without warning amongst the steep cliffs of the east coast. The northern Cleveland Escarpment, which rises from the Cleveland Plain to nearly 1,500 feet, offers one of the grandest sights. But on the high tops the views are almost monotonous, for the moors seem limitless. The southern part is known as the Tabular Hills and consists of older limestones and grits from which the sandstone that still covers the northern moors has been stripped by erosion. Driving from Pickering, in the south, to Whitby, one is immediately aware of the contrast between these grassy limestone hills and the darker moorland beyond. The Moors owe their appearance to the cumulative scouring of season after season of meltwater floods towards the end of the Ice Age. Vast lakes were pent up against the Cleveland Hills, and, as these overflowed, the many valleys running north to south were widened and deepened out of all proportion to the streams which now fill them.

The whole of the moorland area was once forested, but successive clearances have resulted in impoverished soils and the accumulation of up to thirty feet of peat cover. Now

Previous page Heather encircling the Hole of Horcum, on Levisham Moor near Saltersgate, a great natural hollow gouged out by rivers of glacial melt water as they poured down from the lakes that were formed in Eskdale after the last Ice Age. In its cool depths are said to grow ferns that only grow in the Arctic, and legend has attributed the hole to the mythical giant Wade who dug it in order to throw earth at his hapless wife Bell: one of the great clods he flung landed nearby to form the 800 feet high hilltop of Blakey Topping.

Left Walkers pause to enjoy a drift of wild native daffodils on the banks of the River Dove in Farndale, north of Kirkbymoorside.

The crypt below St Mary's Church at Lastingham, believed to have been built over the grave of St Cedd, a Lindisfarne monk who founded a monastery here in 659. The monastery was sacked by the Danes in 866 and refounded in 1078 by Abbot Stephen of Whitby, who built the crypt as a pilgrims shrine. It is unusual in being a self-contained church, distinct from the medieval parish church above it.

A member of the quoits team at Beck Hole, near Goathland, eyes up the lie of the quoits in the clay bed, known as the 'box', into which they are pitched. Eleven or so yards away is another 'box' and both contain a short iron post (the 'hob'). The game of quoits is similar to bowls in that it relies on accurate pitching and a great deal of tactical thinking. The point of the game (believed to have been thought up by blacksmiths' lads who joined two horseshoes together to form rings) is not so much to pitch the heavy iron ring so that it lands over the 'hob' as to block the opponent from successfully doing so. The winning player, or pair of players, is the one whose quoit finishes up nearest to or actually over the 'hob'. The last quoit over the 'hob' is the one that scores, any others being discounted. A good player can dislodge a quoit which rests on the 'hob' and replace it with his own. At Beck Hole, where the pitch has existed since 1882, the first prize in the annual Open Championship has traditionally been a copper kettle, and the matches are fiercely competitive with teams from all over the moors taking part.

the moors only support heather, bracken and rough pasture, whilst the limestone hills have been turned into vast commercial forestry plantations. During the prehistoric period the Tabular Hills and moorland tops were farmed by early settlers who left behind them a rich variety of burial mounds, clearance cairns, earthworks and habitation sites.

Although for much of the year the mood of the moors is one of desolation and bleakness – hence their old name of Blackamoor – they wear a gayer face for a brief period in late August and early September when the heather is in full bloom. But if you abandon the tops for the valleys that divide them you enter a completely different world, where each dale has a character of its own. There is broad Bilsdale, steep and craggy Newtondale with its steam railway, verdant Farndale with its lovely River Dove and meadows carpeted with wild daffodils, and the Forge Valley where the infant Derwent flows through shady woodland. Travel down Ryedale from the heights of Black Hambleton through the beautiful country of Arden to the imposing ruins of Rievaulx Abbey, then go north again along the length of Rosedale, past the stark remains of the once-great ironstone industry and up again onto the dark moorland expanse of Rosedale Head, leaving a coin for poor travellers at the base of Young Ralph Cross.

The Vale of Pickering lies to the south of the Moors. Once a great lake formed by melting glaciers, it is now rich arable land whose autumn fields are stacked with bales of straw after the harvest. To the west of the Vale the foothills of the Hambletons around Kilburn, Wass, Oldstead and Coxwold are a delight; though few sights are more exhilarating than a first glimpse of the great Rose Window of Byland Abbey. Finally there are the gentle Howardian Hills, with their distant views across the old Forest of Galtres towards the towers of York Minster and the incomparable gem of Castle Howard.

Above The view from the edge of Easby Moor across the Cleveland Plain to the escarpment of the Cleveland Hills, the north-western edge of the North York Moors. The name Cleveland comes from the Norse *Klifland*, meaning 'land of the cliffs' and it is easy to see why. The escarpment is the result of a massive geological uplift caused by the residual shock waves of the distant mountain-building activity that formed the Alps, some 40 million years ago. After the last Ice Age the melting glaciers deposited a layer of boulder clay 200 feet thick over the basement rocks of the Plain, thus reducing the height of the escarpment but creating the fertile arable land that is such a feature of the Cleveland Plain. From left to right the peaks of the escarpment are Hasty Bank (the Wainstones), Cold Moor, Cringle Moor, Carlton Moor and Near Moor.

Left The 50 feet high Captain Cook Monument on the edge of Easby Moor. It was erected in 1827 by Robert Campion, a Whitby banker, and today dwarfs the tiny signpost marking the Cleveland Way, an ancient high-level track. The Monument overlooks the Cleveland Plain and the village of Great Ayton where the great explorer (1728-1779) attended school. He was born not far away at Marton, a village now engulfed by Middlesbrough.

Top Known as the 'Yorkshire Matterhorn' because of its unusual shape, the 1057 feet high Roseberry Topping is a landmark of the northern moors. It lies on the Cleveland border offering expansive views, including one of the incongruous urban sprawl of Middlesbrough (on the left). The discovery of ironstone led to extensive mining, which eventually caused the collapse of one side, resulting in its famous outline.

Above Looking down over the hill-farming village of Hawnby towards Upper Ryedale, Great Arden Moor and the distant Hambleton Hills. Rising on the Cleveland Hills, Ryedale is arguably one of the gentlest and most immediately attractive of the dales in the North York Moors area. The road into the dale from Osmotherley drops down into pleasant woodland country around Hawnby before entering the lower dale near Rievaulx.

The ruins of the Abbey of Rievaulx, '*the valley of the Rye*', endowed in 1131 by Walter L'Espec, Lord of Helmsley, and built by Cistercians from Clairvaux in France. It was the first Cistercian abbey in Yorkshire and over the ensuing century became one of the largest, supporting 640 monks. The nave, overlooking extensive remains of domestic buildings, still stands to its full height and is older than any remaining in France. The hardworking monks developed 6,000 acres of pasturage on the uplands of North East Yorkshire, growing wealthy on the wool produced by 14,000 sheep. They also mined iron, made salt, fished, farmed and built watermills and bridges – changing the face of Yorkshire forever.

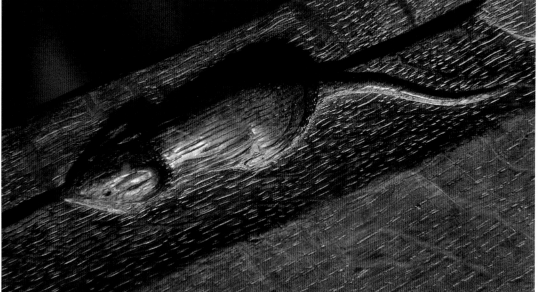

The village of Kilburn in the Hambleton Hills was the birthplace and lifelong home of one of the county's most celebrated craftsmen, the wood-carver and furniture-maker Robert Thompson (1876-1955) who revived the medieval tradition of fine wood carving with hand tools, and whose father was the village wheelwright. He gathered around him a small group of craftsmen and fine examples of his work can be seen in Westminster Abbey, in York Minster, and virtually everywhere else in Yorkshire – particularly in the county's remarkable stock of churches – each identified by the characteristic carved mouse which has earned him the epithet of 'The Mouseman'.

Right Winter sun bathes the creamy sandstone ruins of Byland Abbey on the edge of the Hambleton Hills. In 1134 monks from Savigny in France, by way of Furness Abbey in Cumberland, set out to found a new monastery and finally settled at what was then 'a sodden and scrub-covered site' forty-three years later, and after several false starts. Once boasting the largest Cistercian church in England, the remains include no less than five chapels, extensive cloisters and superb green and yellow glazed floor tiles. The most prominent feature is the west wall of the church, broken by the remains of a magnificent rose window, 26 feet in diameter. In 1322 Byland was ransacked by the Scots after Edward II left supplies here during his ill-fated attempt to invade Scotland. Peace returned until the Abbey was dissolved by Henry VIII.

Below Shandy Hall at Coxwold, on the edge of the Hambleton Hills, once home to the novelist Laurence Sterne who became vicar here in 1760. In its small study he wrote *The Life and Opinions of Tristram Shandy, Gentleman*, the first of the great English novels, as well as *A Sentimental Journey Through France and Italy*. It was whilst in London for the publication of the latter, in 1768, that he contracted influenza and died. He was buried in Bayswater where his body remained until 1969 when it was brought to Coxwold churchyard. The village itself was an estate village of Newburgh Priory, said to be the burial place of the headless body of Oliver Cromwell.

Right The parlour of a reconstructed cottage from Harome at the Ryedale Folk Museum at Hutton-le-Hole on the Tabular Hills between Pickering and the Moors. The cottage is two hundred years old and has an interior which has been 'modified' to the style of a late nineteenth century farm dwelling with kitchen and parlour. Both rooms have ranges, the one in the kitchen designed to burn peat collected from the surrounding moors. On the floor can be seen a 'clipped rug' made from strips of old garments poked through a hessian backing, the making of which was a popular winter pastime.

Sunlight breaking through clouds illuminates the
fertile Vale of Pickering. The green Vale, dotted
with patches of yellow oilseed rape, divides the
Moors from the Wolds and stretches from the
Howardian Hills in the west to the coast near Filey.
After the Ice Age, the torrents of melt water which
carved out the deep valleys of the North York
Moors and the Tabular Hills above Helmsley and
Pickering were pent up in the Vale to form a
massive lake. On its shores the hunter-gatherers of
the Middle Stone Age built seasonal settlements.
The lake finally dried up, leaving in its wake some
of the north's finest agricultural land.

Thin winter light picks out a detail of the superbly carved thirteenth century gateway to Kirkham Priory on the wooded banks of the Derwent near Malton. Above the statues of St Philip, St Bartholomew and Christ are a series of important examples of early heraldic art, the arms of the de Roos, Scrope, de Fortibus, L'Espec, Vaux, de Clar, and Fitz Ralph families – as well as those of England. The Augustinian Priory was reputedly endowed in about 1125 by Walter l'Espec in memory of his son, who died after falling from his horse. The Priory is now ruinous, although part of the nave is still standing, as is the prior's accomodation, the infirmary, chapter house and superbly masoned main drain. Also of note is a sumptuously appointed *lavatorium* where the monks washed their hands before eating.

The Priory Church of St Mary at Old Malton in the Vale of Pickering, comprising the remains of the once great church belonging to the Gilbertine Priory founded here in about 1150. The rest of the original building was destroyed after the Dissolution. On the bank of the River Derwent is Malton itself, its strategic position accounting for the Roman fort of *Derventio*. It is also commercially important, being surrounded by the rich farmland of the Vale of Pickering.

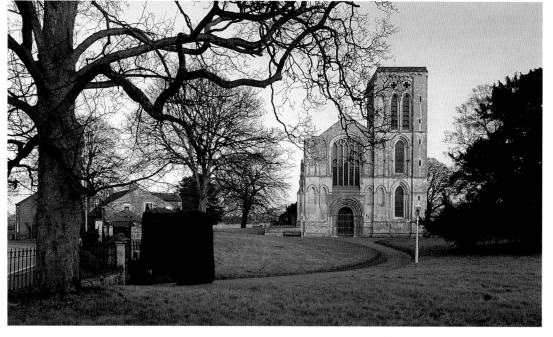

Above Castle Howard, from across the North Lake, of which Horace Walpole wrote in 1772 'I have seen gigantic palaces before but never a sublime one'. Set in the gentle Howardian Hills above the Vale of Pickering, it was originally the site of Henderskelfe Castle, which was bought by Charles Howard (1674-1738), 3rd Earl of Carlisle, a powerful Whig courtier and First Lord of the Treasury. After a dispute over pay with architect William Talman he engaged soldier-playwright John Vanbrugh to design what became one of England's finest Palladian buildings. Vanbrugh began work, on what was incredibly his first building, in 1701 with Nicholas Hawksmoor as supervisor. The 320 feet long Great Hall (right) was the first private English house to have a dome. The house contains many priceless treasures – porcelain, tapestries, furniture – as well as paintings by Gainsborough, Rubens and Holbein. The 1000 acres of parkland include garden temples, fountains, bridges and a mausoleum in which the Earl was interred after his death in 1738. The setting for the television series 'Brideshead Revisited', the house is still the family home of the Howards.

Left The shattered keep of Helmsley Castle rising above the busy market town of Helmsley on the banks of the River Rye. The purple flowers in the foreground are Fairy Foxgloves, planted here by a botanist in the 1930s. The Castle was begun in the twelfth century by Robert de Roos, a northern baron who helped defeat the Scots at the Battle of the Standard in 1138. Modifications continued into the sixteenth century, although its only recorded siege was in 1644 when it held out for three months against Parliamentarian Sir Thomas Fairfax. After its surrender the Castle was largely dismantled.

Below The ruins of Pickering Castle, occupying a rocky prominence of the Tabular Hills which juts out into the narrow valley of Pickering Beck. On the surrounding hillside is built the old coaching and market town known as the 'Gateway to the Moors'. Below is the old Roman road running north across the moors and south to Malton across the Vale of Pickering. William the Conqueror built a motte-and-bailey here after his 'Harrying of the North' and it was subsequently rebuilt in stone by Henry II in the 1220s. The Castle served mainly as a hunting lodge and administrative centre for the surrounding Royal Forest of Pickering and was visited by many medieval English kings. Although the Castle was ruinous by the time of Henry VIII parts of the Forest remain to this day in royal hands.

Left A scene from the superb series of mid-fifteenth century wall paintings which adorn the nave in the Church of Saints Peter and Paul, Pickering. Subjects include St Christopher and St George, the martyrdoms of St Thomas á Becket and St Edmund, the Life of the Virgin Mary, the Passion of Christ and the Seven Acts of Mercy. The characters of Herod's Feast (pictured here) wear fifteenth century costume with Herod identified by his dark, evil face, whilst in front is the dancing Salome holding the head of St John the Baptist. In the characteristic manner of medieval wall paintings the stories are told in the form of highly stylized images in cartoon strip fashion. During the Commonwealth period the scenes were considered idolatrous and whitewashed over. Only in 1851 were they rediscovered, to be restored in 1878.

Above Combine harvesters bringing in the harvest near Whenby, where the undulating Howardian Hills fall away to the Vale of York, a gentle patchwork of fields dotted with red-tiled farmhouses giving the landscape its character.

Left A row of cottages in the quiet village of Terrington, on the edge of the southern escarpment of the Howardian Hills. Now a part of the Castle Howard Estate, Terrington pre-dates the Norman Conquest and its church contains Anglo-Saxon masonry. Its attractive Georgian and Victorian houses with their characteristic red tiles are set back from the main street and fronted with open grass verges.

THE YORKSHIRE COAST

'South wind souther
Blow father home to mother'
Old Yorkshire Fishing Rhyme

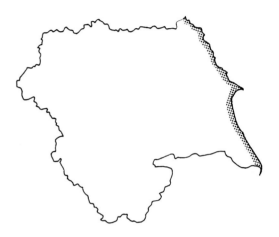

YORKSHIRE's coastline is one of its glories, providing a number of quite different types of fine scenery in its hundred mile course from the heights of Boulby Cliff in the north to the southern mudflats of Spurn. As is so often the case in the county, its geology holds the key to understanding its character. The northern section (from Boulby to Filey) reflects the rocks of the North York Moors with a mixture of sandstones, fossil-bearing unstable shales and ironstones. The southern section (from Bempton to Spurn) consists of a band of chalk around Flamborough, followed by low cliffs of glacial boulder clay.

The high 660 feet cliffs at Boulby on the Cleveland border have been mined for potash and alum shales since at least the sixteenth century, but the first village encountered is the delightful old world fishing community of Staithes, where the young explorer, James Cook, served behind the counter in a little grocer's shop near the storm-battered 'Cod & Lobster Inn'. The ferocity of the sea on this wild coastline is legendary: one wild night a bowsprit crashed through the window of the inn's snug little bar as a ship was dashed against the harbour wall. Port Mulgrave was where ironstone was once shipped from the mines on the Moors, and at Runswick Bay is another little fishing village, its houses seemingly stacked one on top of the next up the steep cliff.

The broad sweep of Sandsend Bay ends at Whitby. Here on the lofty headland above the mouth of the Esk stands the Abbey founded by St Hilda, where England's first poet, Caedmon, dreamed his dreams and where Bram Stoker set his chilling tale of *Dracula*. In the immediate vicinity of Whitby jet has been mined since prehistoric times and a highly profitable industry grew up around it in the Victorian period. Whitby was also home to a large whaling fleet, and a shipbuilding and maritime tradition preserved in the sepia prints of local photographer Frank Meadow Sutcliffe.

The best way to see this coast is to walk the Cleveland Way along the high clifftops, occasionally descending to the numerous little inlets, or 'wykes', that punctuate the cliffs. At the great Victorian spa town and resort of Scarborough, its magnificent castle crowning the headland, one is again in a different world. Between Scarborough and Filey campers and caravanners predominate, with seemingly every foot of the clifftop devoted to the holiday villages and chalets which earn the area the bulk of its income. But the modern visitors enjoys much the same pleasures as his forefathers, and for several centuries and generations of Yorkshire people a day at the seaside has always meant a trip to Whitby, Scarborough, Filey or 'Brid'.

After Filey the coast begins to change. Dazzling white chalk cliffs at Speeton and Bempton are home to immense flocks of seabirds, including puffins, guillemots,

Previous page Lobster pots at Runswick Bay, overgrown with bindweed. With over-fishing on a massive scale, stocks of North Sea herring have been sadly depleted, bringing to an end a way of life that once supported communities like Runswick Bay.

Right Boulby Cliffs on the border of North Yorkshire with Cleveland, and said to be the burial place of the legendary sixth century hero Beowulf. At 660 feet they are the highest on England's east coast. The cliffs are made of alum shale, mined until 1873, which on occasion ignites, producing eerie plumes of smoke. On the left are the twin chimneys of Boulby Potash Mine, one of the deepest in Europe with a mine shaft of 4000 feet.

Below The village of Staithes, built along a creek cut through steep cliffs by Roxby Beck as it flows down from Roxby High Moor to the sea. On either side are precipitious sandstone cliffs, or 'nabs', often covered in seabirds. The name Staithes, pronounced 'steers', means a jetty or landing, and it was in this once busy fishing port that the explorer Captain James Cook (1728-1779) served his apprenticeship to a local grocer and draper before leaving for Whitby and putting to sea. Fishing in Staithes is today limited to inshore crab and lobster potting.

kittiwakes and the only mainland gannet colony in Britain: once gangs of 'climmers' descended the cliffs in rope cradles to gather the gulls eggs that were a delicacy in these parts. From the clifftop at Flamborough, near the light which guides shipping away from the hazards of the coast, the view across the sands of Bridlington Bay is a very different coast. In the haze, the line between sea and land is uncertain, so low are the 'cliffs'. Between Bridlington and Spurn the coast rarely breaches the eighty feet contour, and its vulnerability to erosion is everywhere clearly apparent. Since Roman times more than 75,000 acres have been carried off by the waves: a strip of land one mile deep, where once stood over twenty-five villages.

Hornsea is well-known for its pottery, and as the site of the only remaining freshwater Mere to survive from the post-glacial period when Holderness was dotted with lakes. The resort of Withernsea is popular with the inhabitants of nearby Hull, but its lighthouse is now half-a-mile inland and marooned amid housing. The Yorkshire coast ends at the tip of the two mile long sand spit that leads to Spurn Point – surely the most exposed and solitary spot in the entire county. With the cold, grey North Sea on one side and the muddy waters of the Humber on the other – filled with shipping waiting for a pilot to board and set a course for Hull or Goole – the 'broad acres' seem a world away and you know only too well that this indeed is the very end of Yorkshire.

Fishing and pleasure boats pulled up on the beach at Runswick Bay, once an important seafaring village protected from northerly gales by the headland of Lingrow Cliffs. The name indicates its Viking origins, and in later times it was a centre for the smuggling activities which were rife on this coast. In 1682 the village slipped into the sea, after which the present series of perched cottages were built across the wooded slope. Although fishing continues, many of the houses are now holiday homes, tourists being attracted by the fine sweep of sand.

Boat builder Tony Goodall at work on a traditional wooden hull in his workshop at Sandsend. As well as constructing the occasional new boat, he also repairs old craft, including the Yorkshire 'coble'. The coble is unique to the north-east, being a clinker-built craft descended from the Viking longship. It has a deep bow, high shoulders and a long sloping stern ideally suited to inshore coastal fishing. Like so many of the traditional craftsmen of Yorkshire, Tony Goodall is one of the last of his kind.

Below Oak-smoked kippers at Fortune's of Whitby, an old-established smokery tucked away on Henrietta Street at the feet of the East Cliff. Their distinctive colour and taste is the result of the herring being cured by smoking over oak chippings in a traditional smoking shed, which has been in continuous use for over a century, and whose walls are inches thick with the black resinous deposits from the smoke. The smell of smoke and kippers fills this part of Whitby, and customers come from all over the world to buy Fortune's Kippers.

Above Coloured beach huts line Whitby Sands, which run for three miles from the West Pier to the appropriately named Sandsend in the distance. Strong north-easterly gales make the exposed coast a hazard for shipping, leading to countless wrecks. The lifeboatmen of Whitby have earned more RNLI Gold Medals for gallantry than any other crew in Britain. The town has a long tradition of seamanship and shipbuilding, and it was here that the young James Cook was apprenticed to a local shipowner before joining the Royal Navy.

Right Jet worker Alec Mackenzie, almost hidden behind his array of tools, assessing the potential of a piece of the raw material in his workshop at the feet of the 199 steps in Church Street, Whitby. Unlike coal, jet is the fossilized remains of only one very specific tree, the ancient ancestor of the Monkey Puzzle Tree, and occurs in discreet veins along the Yorkshire coast, across the Moors and in a few other locations in Europe. Once mined on a fairly extensive scale, it is now hand-picked from the local cliffs after storms. Whitby jet became fashionable when Queen Victoria began wearing it after the death of Prince Albert in 1861, and by the 1870s the manufacture of jet jewellery had become a major industry employing 1400 people. By the 1920s cheap imports of imitation jet – the so-called French jet is in fact glass – and a change in fashion converted it back to a local craft carried on by only a handful of people in the town.

The east end of Whitby Abbey at sunset. It was founded on the clifftop above the town for both men and women in 657 by the Anglian King Oswy after his defeat of the pagan King Penda of Mercia. The first abbess was the Northumbrian princess St Hilda, who is reputed to have cleared the site of snakes and turned them into stone (a local explanation of the fossil ammonites so common in the cliffs). Before being sacked by the Danes in 867 the Abbey was home to both St John of Beverley, and Caedmon, the first English poet, who in it wrote his *Song of Creation* after a dream. It was also the location of the Synod of 664 which fixed the date of Easter and finally established the supremacy of Rome over the old Celtic Church. The present building, refounded in about 1067 as a Benedictine Abbey, fared well until the Dissolution, after which its stones were plundered. During the Great War the remains were bombarded by the German Navy.

The smaller photograph shows a detail of the weather-eroded sandstone masonry on the south side of the Abbey presbytery.

The former fishing village of Robin Hood's Bay, seen here from Stoupe Brow where mounds, once said to be archery butts used by Robin Hood and his men as they practised from the walls of Whitby Abbey, are now known to be Bronze Age barrows. Fact and fiction often interweave the entire length of Yorkshire's coast, but the many smugglers' tales have some foundation in the secret tunnels below the maze of red-tiled fishermens' cottages which seem to tumble down the cliff into the sea.

The palatial Raven Hall Hotel, perched above the nearly 600 feet high sea cliffs of Ravenscar, its castellated Terrace Gardens providing superb views northwards across the sweep of Robin Hood's Bay. The cliffs of Old Peak, or South Cheek, form the southern arm of the Bay and were mined for alum from 1640 to 1862. The Hotel was once a manor house where George III recuperated during his bouts of madness. The difficult and unstable geology thwarted the attempts of a group of Victorian businessmen from Bradford to develop the area as a resort.

The ruins of Scarborough Castle crowning the headland above the South Bay. It was built by William le Gros, Count of Aumale, between 1158-1169, after helping England to victory against the invading Scots in the Battle of the Standard. Henry II refortified it by building the great keep, and its subsequent and turbulent history is memorable for a succession of sieges.

The Grand Hotel, once the largest brick structure in Europe and containing a room for each day of the year, overlooking the harbour and South Bay at Scarborough. Its architect was Cuthbert Brodrick, who had designed Leeds Town Hall, and work began in 1863 on the former sight of lodgings where Anne Brontë had come to die in 1849. Scarborough was originally a seafarer's haven and fishing centre, and its future was assured with the discovery of mineral springs in 1626 and the arrival of sea-bathing a century later. Scarborough, boasted one eighteenth physician who depended on it remaining in fashion, 'cheers the spirits and braces the nerves of Peers as well as Commoners'. The arrival of the railway in 1845 brought all the 'Commoners' he could have wished for, and by the end of the century the town had been transformed into Yorkshire's most famous resort.

The mile long peninsula of rock known as Filey Brigg, jutting out from the northern arm of Filey Bay which it shelters. Local legend says it was constructed by the devil in a vain attempt to build a bridge over the North Sea: in reality it comprises the remains of a primeval coral reef – described locally as a 'scaur'. At low tide it is awash with rock pools, the largest of them being a cave known as the 'Emperor's Bath', where the Roman emperor Constantine is said to have bathed whilst on a visit to his garrison at York.

The curving crescent-shaped sands of Filey Bay, stretching five miles from the bluff at Carr Naze southwards to Speeton Cliffs. It has long been an anchorage, protected from north-easterly gales by Filey Brigg, although the lack of a harbour meant that boats had to be hauled up onto the sands. Like other villages along the coast, Filey augmented its income by means of smuggling. By the eighteenth century it had become a fashionable, if quiet, resort, a role it continues to fulfil.

Left A family seeing off the skipper of the Yorkshire coble *Eventide A* as it leaves Flamborough's South Landing for Bridlington at sunset on a winter's evening. Together with the North Landing it has provided a haven for fishermen since Viking times. England's oldest coal-burning lighthouse, built in 1674, stands on the headland above, but the task of guiding shipping along this treacherous coast is today performed by a modern light.

Below Looking down from the Flamborough headland into Thornwick Bay with Bempton Cliffs beyond. Between Flamborough Head and Filey the chalk of the Yorkshire Wolds finally fades, but its swan-song are a series of high cliffs – at Bempton, Speeton and Buckton – which rise to 443 feet. The structure of this part of the coast is self-evident, with crumbling glacial boulder clay above beds of white chalk and Corallian Limestone. The cliffs are a popular nesting site for thousands of seabirds, especially gannets, whose only breeding colony in England is to be found here.

The west door of the Priory Church at Bridlington which leads into a huge nave (185 feet long), all that remains of a once extensive Augustinian monastery. Founded in the early twelfth century by Walter de Gaunt, whose father had assisted William the Conqueror, the Priory soon became one of the richest in the north, numbering St John of Bridlington as one of its canons. Edward II sought shelter here after his skirmish with the Scots at the Battle of Byland, and Henry V gave thanks in the church for his victory at Agincourt. Although most of the Priory buildings were demolished following the Dissolution in 1539, half of the original length of the nave was spared to serve as the parish church, and this is what remains today.

The harbour at Bridlington, busy with summer visitors, and providing shelter for shipping although, like nearby Filey and Scarborough, its lack of a natural harbour led to the construction of a quay. The Old Town grew up inland around the twelfth century Priory, whereas the coastal development, known as Castleburn and later Quay, looked towards the sea for its prosperity. Sea-bathing became popular in the 1770s and the railway eventually united the two towns, enabling Bridlington to develop as a resort well-known for its sand and amusements.

Above Hornsea Mere, a mile inland from the coast and the last survivor of the many freshwater lakes that were left in the clay of Holderness by the melting glaciers of the Ice Age. Others, for example at Ulrome near Skipsea, have been lost to coastal erosion and drainage. Two miles long and one wide, Hornsea Mere is one of Yorkshire's largest lakes and has long been popular with fishermen, and is also a bird sanctuary where teal and widgeon overwinter. The town of Hornsea was founded on the side of the lake, and has subsequently spread to the coast, becoming a seaside resort famous for its pottery.

Opposite page The Lighthouse, together with the stump of a predecessor, on Spurn Point, a narrow 3 ½ mile long sandy peninsula jutting out into the Humber Estuary. Marking the southernmost tip of the Yorkshire coast, it has been built up by the tidal deposition of sand and mud brought down the coast from the north. A submerged offshore reef protects it from destruction, but over the centuries the shape as well as the extent of the peninsula has changed constantly, due to the interaction of sea currents on the one hand and the silt carried down the Humber Estuary on the

other: as a result, Spurn Point is Yorkshire's most fragile landscape feature. A lifeboat station has existed here since 1810 and today is the last with a live-in crew. The Point is also home to the Humber Pilots, who have guided shipping in the Estuary since an unaccompanied ship floundered during a visit of Henry VIII. Considering its size and exposed position, the peninsula's natural history is remarkable. Waders and seasonal migrants find rich pickings on the mudflats, and sea holly, sea purslane and many other salt-loving plants flourish in the dunes.

THE PHOTOGRAPHS

THE task of producing a photographic portrait of the vast County of Yorkshire was a stimulating if daunting prospect. On the one hand it gave me the opportunity to systematically explore the 'Broad Acres' in a way I had not been able to do before; on the other the amount of travelling involved and my dependence on weather which in Yorkshire is at best fickle was at times intimidating: many places had to be visited several times, others were plagued by scaffolding or traffic. The photographic archive I have built up over some ten years of wandering about the Dales provided the foundations for the first two sections of the book, though a lot of the photographs are recent and were specifically taken. The rest were taken over the course of a little more than a year, during which time I travelled nearly 8,000 miles, shot 366 rolls of film and produced over 3,000 transparencies - from which we painstakingly and agonisingly made our final selection.

The subjects we have elected to portray are, to a great extent, a matter of personal choice, and the constraints imposed by the size and price of the final book. Inevitably there is much we have had to omit. Even a book twice the length of this one would fail to do justice to a county as vast and as varied as Yorkshire. We believe, however, that we have gone a fair way towards providing a real portrait of Yorkshire's character, its people as well as the places.

All the photographs were taken using a Bronica SQA Medium Format (2¼″ square) SLR camera, using 40mm, 50mm, 80mm, 150mm and 250mm Zenzanon lenses. Over 90% of the photographs are on Fujichrome Velvia (50ASA) film; the remainder being on Fujichrome RDP, RDPII and RHP (100 and 400ASA) film, with a mere handful on Ektachrome EPR (64ASA). The rest of my equipment consisted of a Benbo 2 Tripod, HiTech graduated neutral density and 'warming' (81-series) filters and polarizing filters. I have only used flash where it was absolutely essential.

I would also like to thank John Edenbrow (Leeds) and Walter Scott Postcards (Bradford), for allowing the inclusion of two photographs taken for other projects, and Leeds Photovisual and Chromagene for supplying film stock, equipment and E6 processing.

Discovering the incredible diversity and richness of Yorkshire has been a remarkable experience. My love and respect for the Dales has not been diminished, but my horizons have been broadened immeasurably and my knowledge of the landscape, history and heritage of the rest of the county has grown as a consequence. My greatest pleasure has been meeting the people of Yorkshire, many of whom have made a contribution to what appears in these pages. To all those I have met along the way I would like to extend my thanks: it is to them that these pictures are dedicated. My thanks also to the landladies who have given me hospitality and fine breakfasts, and all my friends for their support, encouragement and sustenance.

TREVOR CROUCHER

ACKNOWLEDGEMENTS

MANY people have helped to create this book, and our thanks are due to them all. First and foremost, there are the people of Yorkshire who are depicted in the book, either wittingly or unwittingly. Then there are those, listed below, who have most generously helped with the provision of access, co-operation and arrangements.

Colin Gray, Eric Sanderson, Eric Thompson, John Morley, Bill Cockerill and David Hoggard (Beck Hole Quoits Team); David Thornton (verger of Beverley Minster); Dick Wood (Bradshaw Mummers); Robin Sharpe (Bridlington Priory); Mrs Susan Cunliffe-Lister and Josie Harrison (Burton Agnes Hall); James Sanderson, John Sanderson and Beverley Kilvington (Catterick Racecourse); Mark Graham, Dave Haywood, Jill, Cliff and David Harrison (Conisbrough Castle); David Hughes (Courage Breweries, Staines, Middx); Siobhan Kirrane (Craven Museum, Skipton); John Rowland, Gary Wells, Jayne Warrender and Douglas Mitchell (Davy Roll Company, Sheffield); Paul Harper and Glynn Davis (Yorkshire Bank, Doncaster); Leigh Hales (Flamborough); Susan Walshaw and C. C. Hitch (Gawthorpe); Ray Ellison (Grenoside Sword Dancers); Mr G. Long (The Harewood House Trust Ltd); A.O. Hunt (Harewood Steam Rally); the staff of Holyrood House, Hedon; Gladys Cook, Mary Collinson and Michael Hickes (Hemingbrough Minster); Geoff Morton, Mark Morton and William Castle (Hasholme Carr Farm, Holme upon Spalding Moor); John Hodgson for the map on page 6; Peter Wells (Holme Spinning Co., Bradley); Tom Prime (Kiplin Hall); Pat, Trevor and Michael Weighell (Kirkby in Cleveland); John Bade (Victoria Quarter, Leeds); Flt Lt Maggie Pleasant, Flt Lt Al Shinner and Cpl Richard Massey (RAF Leeming); David Taylor, John Taylor, Albert Mawson and Geoff Dunn (Malham Lamb Sale); Alan Houghton, Ian Carpenter, Clive Ponder, Alan Daintee, Dennis Bagshaw and Mick Burrell (Maltby Colliery); Kenneth Murray (Naburn Lock); Ann Kitching (Pickering); Duncan Ritson (Pickering Castle); Patrick Cooper and John Grainger (The Stewart Trust, Burnby Hall, Pocklington); Tony Dunn, Keith Worden and Ted Dodsworth (Ripon); Martin Watts, Dorothy Ellison and Helen Mason (Ryedale Folk Museum); Tony Goodall and Maurice Brown (Sandsend); Marion Cockrem (Beck Hole); Anne Laycock (Seaton Ross); Jean and Ron Gulliver (Sheffield); Jenny Kirk (Sheffield); Trevor Smith (Sheffield); Clive Bowes (Skidby Windmill); Sir Tatton Sykes, Michael Kenneally and Ann Hines (Sledmere House); Fred Knights (Sowerby Bridge); Yvonne Clark and Jocelyn Appleyard (Stillingfleet); Wendy and Des Waslin (Walkington); Roger Dower, Susan Jones, John Merrick, Gordon Rush, Arthur Lumb and Lesley Denneny (Walkley Clogs, Hebden Bridge); Alice Amsden and Richard Clarke (Wensleydale Creamery); John Ambler (Fitzwilliam Estate, Wentworth Woodhouse); Jean Davies (Whitby); Alec MacKenzie, Hal and Debbie Redvers-Jones (Victorian Jet Workshop, Whitby); Barry Brown (Fortune's Kippers, Whitby); The National Railway Museum, York.

Our final thanks are to our publisher David Burnett, without whom none of this would have been possible.

DUNCAN SMITH AND TREVOR CROUCHER

INDEX

The City of Ripon Morris Dancers during the annual feast of St Wilfred, Ripon.